HIPPIE MEMOIRS

HIPPIE MEMOIRS

SANTA FE DAYS

CLIFF ALEXANDER

CITI OF
BOOKS

CITIOFBOOKS, INC.
3736 Eubank NE Suite A1
Albuquerque, NM 871113579
www.citiofbooks.com
Hotline: 1 (877) 3892759
Fax: 1 (505) 9307244

Ordering Information:

Quantity sales. Special discounts are available on quantity purchases by corporations, associations, and others. For details, contact the publisher at the address above.

Printed in the United States of America.

| ISBN13: | Softcover | 979-8-89391-276-0 |
| | eBook | 979-8-89391-277-7 |

Library of Congress Control Number: 2024916992

TABLE OF CONTETNS

i

CHAPTER 1

Who Slammed on the Brakes?

I couldn't help but wonder how I got here, on the screened-in porch of the hepatitis wing at the Fort Collins Army Hospital. The wind was drifting through the trees rustling leaves and spinning up dust and papers; the smell of fresh cut grass wafted through the screens. A soldier riding a mower back and forth brought back memories of me pushing a mower a long childhood ago.

The hospital porch was a lot better than the stockade, I had to admit. These days had become blurred together. Factors out of my control had spun into motion—as if I were floating down the Colorado River hearing giant rapids just ahead: I was caught and there was nothing I could do.

The company commander had already known I wasn't going to put on the uniform. I had been clear about that. I had told him that I felt okay wearing my corpsman whites, and I thought we had a sort of a deal until my conscientious objector discharge came through. So, when he called me down and gave me the direct order to put on my fatigues, I was surprised. And even more so, after I said I wouldn't, when the orderly came out of the office with a loaded shotgun.

The cuffs were pretty tight, I kept thinking on the way to the stockade. There was a no-turning-back feel to all of this—a deep-water feel one gets after the undertow has taken over. It had been the Friday before the scheduled brigade inspection. Okay, so I had this idea to put up pictures from the Mỹ Lai Massacre on the inside of my locker, the way others had their Playboy pinups—but there was no way they could have known.

I sat there in my whites, handcuffed, looking down at the shiny black tile as the paperwork got stamped and signed, and the orderly left giving me a last hard look of disdain. The cuff's edges were biting into my skin. I couldn't help but see the humor in it. Here a conscientious objector being cuffed like a common criminal, but, hey, the dye was being cast, and it felt like that dye was me.

I hadn't thought anything about being assigned to an empty barracks. That night just before the 11-to-7 shift guard came on, the black guard had tried to level with me. "You really should put that uniform on," he had said with a tone of concern that I didn't really understand—that was until the other guard showed up.

"What?" he had interrupted when I had started to explain I was a conscientious objector. And "You one of those hippie peace marijuana smokers. I got some news for you, put the uniform on," he said. He raised his fist, serious intent on his face. There wasn't even an ounce of faking. I felt the impact and slammed against a bunk behind me.

"What?" he said, "I didn't hear you." He grabbed me, raising his fist again putting his ear toward me. I didn't say anything. "Okay then, this is for Jack who got shot out in the boonies so you can disrespect the uniform. No, I don't think so." His fist shot out. My left cheek felt the impact, and I went sprawling backwards. "Why, you're unfit to wear it, but by God, you're going to put it on." He said with his voice getting tight.

I could feel his hand on my chest as he clutched at my corpsman white smock, ripping it. I raised my hand feebly. I was beaten. I caught the bundle of green rolled up fatigues he threw at me and started to change.

"You're lucky," he said. "I just had a fight with the wife, and I could have worked you over all night just to let off some steam." There was a matter-of-fact tone to his voice that had shifted from the emotional tone he had just before. "So, you better keep your yap shut, or I just might work you over now because I feel like it."

For the rest of the night I lay on the cot, scared stiff that something might set him off. I was so scared that the fact that I was wearing the green fatigues hadn't even bothered me. The next day I was glad to see the sun come up.

When the new guard came on, he asked, "Any problems?"

"Nope, he just needed a good reason to put on the uniform, and I gave him one." He said looking over at me.

The guard looked at my bruised face and looked back without saying anything.

It was then I touched my left cheek and could feel that it was swollen pretty badly. I became aware of the ache that came on as a throb.

About then the loudspeaker sounded. "Private Alexander is needed at the main command post."

"That you?" the new guard asked.

"Yes," I said.

"Yes what?" he said raising his voice.

"Yes, sergeant," I said louder.

3

"Fall in behind," he muttered just loud enough for me to hear.

On the way over I glanced through the chain link and could see a new yellow Cadillac. The ace up my sleeve was that I had hired a civilian lawyer from Cherry Creek in Denver. I had got his name from an anti-war rally led by Joan Baez and her then-spouse David, which I had attended in Boulder. David had on rimless glasses with a slanted cut in them, and his hair was already thinning. He had a quiet- martyr attitude about him, as he spoke about facing the three years in prison that he was getting ready to serve.

When I had told him my particular dilemma, he slid a business card into my hand. That card was the reason I was now on my way to the main command post. I took a deep breath, as they opened the first set of gates and I walked past MPs in starched uniforms with their shiny forty-fives fastened to their belts. They were not screwing around; this was all business. I had that cog-in-the-wheel feeling, as I stepped up to the door of the main office. Inside I saw Dwayne Cassidy, my lawyer, in a light grey suit with a leather brief case. His tan and tight face spoke of country clubs, as well the gravity of the moment that I was finding myself in.

"Is there a room where I can confer with my client?" he asked, with an air that this was a right he knew full well they had to accommodate.

A master sergeant motioned in a direction. "Take the first room on the right," he said.

As we walked in, I felt my idea to get him as my lawyer had been a good one.

"Well," he started, "how are you holding up?" He looked at my swollen cheek and the bruise on my chin along with the abrasions.

"I've been in better shape," I added.

"You've got to remember that in here, you're theirs. I can only help you so much. So," he took a deep breath and looked out the window. "Let's see, time-wise, this could draw out for a month or two, so you're going to have to hang in there."

I was hoping to hear something about bail, but then it hit me about last night and how there were no lights on the whole night like the other barracks, and that cold feeling came back. I started rubbing my hands together.

"Hey, look at me," he said in a pleading tone. "Ah, look you're in here because you're following your conscience; you're being true to yourself. That's all I can tell you." As he said it, he looked past me with a distant look that I didn't understand. "Well, I gotta go. I'll file all the papers and," he added getting up and walking to the door, turning and stopping. "Don't go and do anything stupid." He then opened the door and talked to the guard stationed just outside the door. "We're done in here," he said, and just before he headed down the hall, he shot a glance in and gave me a nod.

I leaned back in the chair. The midmorning light was slanting in through the blinds throwing bar-like shadows in front of me. Just what I needed, more reminders of where I was. Okay, I couldn't argue with the being-true-to-myself point, so I sat and mulled that over.

It wasn't long before the door swung open and a black major came in and sat down where my lawyer had been sitting. He was in no hurry to come to his point as he took his time to get comfortable in the chair and crossed his legs. While I was glancing about taking in what I could, I continued to have that blank look on my face. I had already learned that in the yard, or whatever *aka* you use for the stockade, you don't let on to what you're aware of. You don't let them in even a bit, and this was only my second day, and no one told me about this either. You could call this jail-house osmosis.

"You know," he started, "where all this could end up? They have a place in Kansas called Leavenworth and plenty of four-by-eight cells. I've seen plenty like you with your fancy lawyers come and go. Where is he going to be when the real shit hits the fan? He's going to be out shooting a round of golf with his lawyer buddies. That's where." He turned and looked out the window. "Yes, there's nothing like rows of chain link and barb wire. I just love it here."

He walked to the window, scratched at something, and then turned. "Now you, you're different than most of them in here. Hey, I can tell the difference. You, you wouldn't steal if I left a pile of money in here. You could be a real problem, and that's what I don't need. So, tell you what I'm going to do. Let's just say for egging on Sergeant Channing last night and for disobeying a lawful order, your new residence is going to be maximum. That'll keep you out of the regular population. What you say to that, Private Alexander?"

Then just like that, the whirl began again: the shiny floors, white walls, out into the sunshine squinting, following a guard through sets of gates full of chain link and barbed wire, the passwords, up the steps to max, more passwords and reciting of orders, clicking and turning of tumblers of locks and the swinging open of heavy doors, a dark cool hulking presence of space and with adjustment of my retina, a hallway.

"This way, Private," the guard said, walking up to a cell and opening the door. "It's all yours." He added with no emotion. I could just make out a bunk on the left and a toilet in the back with no seat. I turned around in time to see the metal door with a set of bars in the middle clank shut.

This was to be home, like the guard said. Two weeks—including three visits to the mental health clinic, a three-day fast that gave me a midnight nosebleed, another visit to mental health, and a referral resulted in me here sitting on this porch of the hepatitis ward. I should be on the mental health ward, but the corpsman there got busted for drugs, or so they told me, and since you are only told what they want you to know, it didn't have to be the truth.

An orderly came to the doorway leading to the porch. "Private Alexander, your lawyer is here to see you."

I sauntered behind him in my cloth slippers and the grey bathrobe. Hadn't been a month since I was taking temperature on a malaria ward just down the hallway, I thought, following him to a little room.

A younger man was waiting for me. I didn't recognize him.

"Hello," he said, "Dwayne couldn't make it. He is in court right now. I'm his junior associate, and I have just come from the adjutant's office. I've got some good news. I was able to cut you a deal. If you plead guilty to disobeying a lawful order, then you will be able to get out with a general discharge." He said smiling, proud of the news he was delivering.

"But," I stumbled with my thinking. I had envisioned pleading guilty à la Gandhi and becoming a great martyr for the anti-war movement. Caving in just hadn't been part of what I had gone through.

"I know," he interrupted, "but this way you can have benefits to go to school, as well as some other ones. Let's see," he stopped and began thinking as if he had not even contemplated this option would even be needed going over. "Otherwise, you're theirs and they could give you three years. So, think about it. We go in there with what we've got, and there's not much more I can do for you. Right now, they want to be done with this, and that's our leverage."

All he had said was right, but I felt like I was selling out. "Okay," I said. "Let's go with it."

"Then here," he said, pushing some papers toward me. "Sign right there," he added, pointing to an open place on the form. Just like that, a different set of wheels were set to motion. Two more weeks of revolving my day around the life on the ward til another guard showed up with another set of papers that read Discharge Papers on the top. I had to get about ten signatures from various places until the final signature and the stamp came down hard on the bottom of the page.

I rode out of the fort on the bus—a free man. Well, free from the stockade but with a new set of bars I had never even considered before. I was now a man with a stain that no one could see.

I went up to Boulder but nothing was the same. The simple drinking days had, for some reason, gone. I was a duck out of water, a lizard in a blizzard, a horse in the middle of the ocean. No matter where I went or what I did, I couldn't shake it. I wandered over to the library and got a spot in the magazine section and tried to take stock. Reading about other people took some of the pain away. There was a *Look* magazine article on Santa Fe and how there were communes where people could fit in. Going home was out of the question since Dad had sold the ranch in Paonia, Colorado, and had relocated with Mom to Niceville, Florida, (on the Panhandle) and had worked a lifestyle around the ocean going out on his boat and fishing. It was not a hard call for me.

Waking up after sleeping rough at Chautauqua Park in Boulder, shivering under a worn-out army blanket, began it all, as unconscious as it could be. Not feeling any different under my dark cloud, I walked toward the Denver-Boulder Turnpike, feeling momentum in my steps that I wasn't used to.

The sky was breaking into clear blue, as the city was beginning to stir with the hum of cars heading to their eight-o'clock shifts. I raised my right arm and stuck out my thumb. It wasn't some Zen realization. Something subtle, as if not at all, yet it was. In one heartbeat, just like the moment a seed springs to life; so that, thereafter there is no turning back. Destiny was the thrill I was feeling, and keys were turning inside of me, lining up the tumblers that had been holding me back, as I scanned ahead projecting my best first impression to the oncoming drivers.

Then, just like that, it happened.

CHAPTER 2

No Holding Back

My Fate is In the Wind

In that moment, I found that I couldn't hold back, going headlong, the swirl was building up quiet momentum so that, if Santa Fe was my true destiny, then it would come, and currents would carry me there, since it was meant to be. In the back of my mind, it was still going to be a long shot; but for now, all I needed was the blue sky and a positive attitude this fearless thumb, a road and my naiveté to back it, squinting out at the onslaught of shiny cars, heading to their silent destinations.

The pieces were there, even if I wasn't seeing them immediately. Couches would always be a conversation away waiting to happen. A place to crash was just a matter of chemistry; that would come in the great scheme—it was really just a matter of being in tune. As I rode, the pavement slid on contours of rolling landscapes inside my retina, mesas ridged in sandstone, buttes in far distances that went from horizon to dusty horizon between one-sided dialogues that never really got heard.

It was now a matter of motion, regarding how to get somewhere among the drawing magnet that kept Santa Fe fresh on my mind. The rides from Boulder fell into place one at a time past Denver. Then I caught a ride out of Castle Rock to Pueblo, then to Raton.

Waiting at Raton

Everything was flowing well until I got to Raton. Funny how the hot sun, with no hat, and seeing rides going by started to eat away my self-confidence, cutting it to the quick. What progress I'd made was beginning to unravel as yesterday snapshots began filling in the void, which never was a problem before, catching me off guard. Vignettes of stockade events ran their way freely into my powerless conscious to run their course and come back around, rendering me weak with the sun on my face and my thumb out. The cars were speeding by my feeble attempt to project a positive image of myself, only now failing badly (the cancelled appointments at the mental health clinic, the guards waiting for an excuse to lay some hurt on me, the guard who'd come in at one a.m. to give me behavioral amotivation). In this swirl of randomness my balance sensed this abyss I was falling into. It occurred to me that stepping into the traffic so oblivion could free me from this sucking chaos. At the same time, the colors of the rolling hills and their sculptured vistas held me captive to stark beauty that ran in all directions, contours rhyming with shadows. Noticing even the smallest hills distracted me from becoming a statistic.

Thirst then took over, stalling out my negation, safe for now from the bottomless pull of my phantoms. The valley expanded into the distance as the tanned hills caught the glare from the sun on the high places where they glowed bright yellow, and underneath edges slanted shadows out cool dark grey. Three-dimensional studies of composition all around me went on and on forever in this beauty. Each hill had this voice talking only to me of its secrets. More unraveled with what my intelligence could discover from hills running and blending and coming back around here to the east, then abutting back toward the

12

slanted west juxtaposed shadows. Where the light struck, I drank of this continuous vision fresh with each new insight.

This me, balanced beside an on-ramp with my thumb out, allowing the spin of all the orbits to play where they would, keeping my discipline to stay safely to the side of the pull, enough so that humor found me breaking a smile, don't jinx it with determination bleeding through the desperation, breaking clean with my thumb up.

Errrrrt, a faded silver Porsche pulled over, skidding as it did.

A Ride

My mouth fell open, hardly believing what I was seeing. I grabbed my pack and ran as fast as I could to the door, opened it and pushed my pack to the back, and got in. *Thank you*, my body language translated with movement, escape from boredom's reason, which was why I was now riding—understood, happy to concur.

"Yes, thanks, I'm going as far as Santa Fe," I blurted out.

"Got family there?" he said, shifting into second gear then third, as I felt my head being pushed into the head rest, as the hefty engine behind me whined at a high pitch like this racehorse was pulling at the bit wanting to go.

"No, just want to see what'll come my way, what I'll discover. I've heard stories of communes and getting high, you know. I've got this good feeling about it and am getting excited."

"Yes, I've wondered about that place myself too," he added, as he navigated a wide turn that ran up then to the southwest over a canyon wash that had an old rusted car body to the right half covered in brown sifted, dunned up, rippled sand.

"Where are you headed?" I asked, glancing at what was left as the car slid quickly out of sight before I could guess the make.

"LA," he said, as he kept his focus on the road's turnings ahead, adding, "Got done with my vacation, visited my dad in Baton Rouge, now I'm going back to the firm I work for."

Cedars and red ridges tufted with sandstone and cedars went by, all held together with the overall weather's story of erosive wear where the weakest point was found by the water's constant touch, gravity guided by how nature found the shortest way to travel. Lines separated as he went along that intrigued my gaze continually, as each blended into another that became like a rhyme of a poem. Pieces all seemed so related that made a certain sense, for the secrets inside the turning relationships— the gathering and breaking apart in the utter randomness of nature that, when I looked closer, showed such rigid exactness in design. Always just a matter of this small lean, just so in raw distinction to make at the moment, traveling quickly by, just enough to fathom.

We continued on, as the rough road swung more toward the west, now going at right angles to most of the gutted washes bone dry, what it is about running north to south that water seems to obey. Passing the Pecos River, as the road swung easily around to a more northwesterly direction, a sudden kick tightened in my chest from deeper inside along with questions about tomorrow's possibilities that lingered. Would it all fall nicely into place or would the disintegrations start? Those dominoes falling backward mixed up my feelings as I got out and thanked him, for saving me back there at Raton.

CHAPTER 3

Santa Fe

The turquoise color of the wide-open sky held me in awe, balanced there beside the overpass road full of anticipation, as an old Chevy pickup came slowly around a bend into view. Somehow as he got closer, the old man at the wheel didn't say a word as he slowed down and then stopped. His easy smile told me all that I needed to know about him, so I put my pack in the back, opened the door and got in, noting this good omen, that was happening out of the blue.

The lines of the man's face spoke of a deep wisdom gained much the same way rings do, telling stories of a mighty tree with the lean thin years right beside the fuller good ones.

We drove up Old Pecos Trail as it wound heading North, and a slender thread weaved inside of me along with the sights of the adobe houses, cobbled streets, past dusty alleys, old shops, aged trees and milling tourists. With the pastel blue sky above, wide winging, feeling free, I felt a peace ring inside. I leaned back looking out with my arm up on the top side of the rusty faded metal.

The old man was whistling a song as he shifted gears. No small talk was needed. He knew he was helping me out and didn't need me to remind him of what was obvious. Passing an alleyway, I spied a group of hippies coming out of a large wooden gate abutted to a high brown stucco wall, and I made a mental note and kept on with my free sightseeing.

"Could you take me by the hospital?" I asked, relaxing more.

He nodded, not missing a beat of the song he was whistling, as state government buildings went by shining white over a canyon wash and then galleries. He slowed as the street curved a northwest as a large white stucco building came up midst rolling lawns. He slowed, down shifting, and pulled to a stop by a large elm. I got out, thanked him, we mirrored two smiles and he left.

I wandered up to the building and around the grassy backside where there was a park that had a high wrought-iron fence, thinking that will do for now. I'll get the interview done later, unafraid since serving as an Army medic would suffice. I headed for an ornate gate in the cool shadows, still struck by the freshness of the robin-egg-blue sky and the coolness of the shade, with the breeze on my arms heading west on the sidewalk that was broken and pushed up here and there by the thick roots of the towering old elm trees.

I followed the overall direction the people were taking to town, and I felt a skip inside open a deeper perception, so that greens got a sharper shade of emerald jade or turquoise. The shops' weathered signs told me of age that revealed deep grains and grooves of wood as I scanned through windows to shelves of kachinas, concho belts, bracelets, bead work, silver buckles, rings, and Navajo rugs that hung on the upper ceiling rafters.

Little by little, I could see the afternoon light was shifting down west so I found myself reversing course back south to the alleyway where the hippies were leaving that courtyard gate. Keeping the deep blue of the mountain to my left, I pushed on, enjoying the fragile yet completely new vistas.

The Commune

With the still-warm August sun angling down, I arrived just in time for watered- down vegetable soup and hot fresh white bread. I sat at a picnic table, eavesdropping on scattered conversations of the coming and going of everyone's busy agenda, full of city slang or country twang—clues childhoods freely give away, as a Jimmy Hendrix album played in the now darkening background, Purple Haze hyphenated with the smell of incense and rustling leaves, between skips in dialogues interrupted by a random question lingering mid-innuendo in the ever-moving glances waiting for eye contact eye, in case the pause could allow a smile or brief hesitation. (What sudden moments could unleash the imagination to run open, how the hormones need little reasons to climb the situation more).

The green branches swayed overhead to the rhythm of the evening, casting the ever-moving dappled shadows on tables and walls, listening between the lines at what never quite got said, playing it safe just audible in the rustle and murmur of different people conversing.

Maybe... Maybe Not

I could make out her face and blonde hair shiny under the lightbulb. The strands were askew, pulled by the breeze across her face, which she would brush absentmindedly back as she caught my gaze with her pouty lips and tanned cheeks that widened as she smiled. Her voice flowed syllables straight from Texas in an unmistakable drawl.

17

"You all don't do things that'a'way where I come from in Abilene." She went on looking directly in the face of a long-haired guy. "No way," she said looking away. "I don't do grass, I don't care, not my style."

A whiff of pot smoke came from an opposite corner of the large patio. The orange tip glowed along with a rushing sucking sound that stopped upon which, the joint was passed to the next who repeated the routine. As that went on, I noticed her take a breath and her blouse went taunt. She was well built and had a doublewide-trailer nobility to her presence in the way she held her head and the straight set of her shoulders. There was no denying that she wasn't going to take shit from anyone.

The conversation muffled with the rustle of the branches overhead in the cool air, savoring this thing freedom, I stretched my arms out and felt the coolness of the night breeze coming from the mountain. I glanced around at the lay out of the patio with the high adobe walls. The south side was where the large wooden gate that I'd seen earlier. Large ornate hinges held the weight with their Spanish workmanship.

I could tell that I was being accepted, so I relaxed and took in the vibes. The one girl had gotten up and was wandering past me to get a refill. As she approached the pitcher of lemonade that was on the main table, she slowed down going past me. "Having a private conversation?" she asked, smiling and putting her hands on the tabletop.

"Oh, no, just enjoying the evening and the cool air," I said, looking up at her. She was prettier than I had expected, looking right into her blue eyes. I smiled, and added, "I hitched most of today so I'm happy to rest."

"You look sunburnt," she said, looking closely at my face.

"Yeah, I learned lessons out there—never be without a hat or water."

"The road will do that to you. That's why I prefer to catch the bus," she added stretching, showing more tautness to her flowered blouse.

"Would you like to sit down?" I asked, hardly believing the words that were coming out of my mouth just as natural as you please.

"Don't mind if I do," she said, rubbing her arms with her hands.

"Cold?" I asked, removing the flannel shirt I had over my regular one. "On the road, you never know when it'll get cold or rain," I said.

She waved it off but I reached over and gave it to her just the same, and as she put it on, I noticed her even features and her pouty pink lips.

Overhead there was now a shard of stars weaving designs of stallions, scepters, fountains and dippers pointing to other stars all billions of light years old, coming at that moment right there. The silence stayed as she settled easily into a good relaxed position.

"Have you checked out the square yet, looked pretty interesting?"

"No, I'm not into beads or pottery," she answered matter-of-factly.

Suddenly, just like that, the gap was there in a cold hard disconnect, my face, body—well curved on the edge of my line of vision all held me, but then something in me said, "I gotta get some rest."

"Where do we sleep?" I asked, looking around at the now quiet patio.

"The men sleep in that part of the hacienda," she said pointing, "and the ladies sleep on that side," she added pointing to the left.

"Thank you, I gotta crash," I said, picking up my backpack.

"Have a good night," she said, lighting up a cigarette and taking a drag.

19

Finding a place easy like this to crash was a really big deal, and a ton of pressure came off me, as I walked to the door and went hesitantly inside the entrance she had politely pointed out.

Okay, so I was abrupt, but her negative attitude had turned me off, looking around, as my eyes adjusted to the dark. There were no beds, just bed rolls here and there randomly placed in a first-come, first-choice way, so I found an open spot. I could not help but smile about my good fortune as I lay there under my blanket, with my hands behind my head.

The Interview

The next day at the hospital, Ms. Albert interviewed me in her starched uniform that rose and fell between her breaths that distracted me right. Her name tag was near the stressed buttons so my concentration shifted into awkwardness as I tried to answer her questions about the where, what's and how's.

"Oh, yes, I worked at the ER at Fort Carson, Colorado, and yes, I could start there right away, if you there is an opening." I paused looking to the safety of her paperclip. My stare stayed away from her reflection on the desk glass as her breathing made alternate pressures to her tight blouse.

She smiled with the corner of her mouth as she spoke, now and then looking away so that I was free to observe her the way women do, when they let you know they know more than they are letting on. She added, "There are openings. Could you start early on Monday? Be here at eight o'clock sharp. Let's see, show up at the main lobby and we'll go from there."

"Do you know where I could get some orderly smocks?" I asked.

She took a deep breath, pointing as she did adding, "It's in that direction about three miles, called Mesa Shopping."

The next day I wandered over, and it was there like she had said. I got a shirt for ten dollars and then just like that I had a job.

Helping Out

The first week, a wrangler who spoke no English, came in hurting. He had an abrasion on his leg from landing on the side of the corral, having been bucked off of a horse he was attempting the break. The wound had reached the state of infection when the dark lines ran up his leg, from the source of this tender swollen jagged cut.

One doctor gave it a cursory glance and prescribed penicillin pills, but in his eyes was a look that said he was in a bad way, so I faked confusion and asked another doctor to come by, which doctor promptly assigned him to be admitted immediately. When the other doctor came back from diagnosing other patients and glanced disdainfully at the now officially signed admittance order, he gave me a look that told me that I had made an enemy that day.

It wasn't long until I fell into the rhythm of the job and my free time. My day started usually at six, when I got myself dressed, ate breakfast and had just enough time to walk from the commune to the hospital and get to the men's locker room to shower with plenty of hot water, then dry off and change into my white pants and hospital smock.

Life on the ER, wherever you are, always has that state of randomness so that you are either standing around bored or in a frantic way trying to find a pulse or blood pressure on a beat-up patient.

CHAPTER 4

The Pieces Begin to Fit

I also figured out the commune fast from my daily observations. A priest wearing a white collar and a black smock came by once a week with an air of authority to check on things. He was one of those guys that had a thick beard and hairy arms. He'd look around pensively, behind his wire-rimmed glasses with his dark sensitive eyes and a thin smile, he seldom used. He never spoke to us everyday folk who needed a place to stay who were mostly crashers, that stayed on for about two days who would move on, only to show up again a week or two later. They used the commune as a base of operations to rely on—it was everyone's plan B that allowed us to freely take chances knowing, if all else failed, there would be a safe place to sleep.

I kept putting twenties anonymously into the collection bottle, and since I was the only one with a job, they had to figure it out, which gave me a feeling, that I could come and go as I wanted. I moved up to the thick rug to sleep on, that was—until I started scratching in my privates continuously the next day.

Lucy, a nurse, noticed my dilemma and said during morning break, "Get Campho-Phenique, and that'll take care of them fast," She said it in an under-the-cuff way that I appreciated.

The ER work went on of sprains, back spasms, cuts, bloody noses, broken arms, busted-up lips or other ailments due to a car wreck that had come in. Off to the X-ray I pushed a gurney with a gasping patient hooked up to an IV, part of the up-and-down roller coaster of any emergency room on any given shift.

Afterwards, I went to Walgreens and got the Campho-Phenique. When I got to the commune, I went to the restroom, ready to see if it was going to work but I had to wait as someone was taking his good time. A glassy-eyed hippie came out and smiled, and looked away. I went in and quickly locked the door then dropped my drawers and liberally applied it to my crotch and could feel the warmth spread its effects. Wham, just like that, the itching ceased. I then cut across the patio toward the sleeping room.

On top of my pack was the shirt that I had loaned out to Susan— that blonde girl with the southern accent I had met the first day. There was a note in the shirt pocket. "Cliff," it read, "thanks for giving me your shirt. One of the few gentlemanly things that have happened to me here. Guess I wasn't cut out to be a hippie. I'm going back to Abilene where I'll go back to being a waitress. Thanks for being nice that night, and not taking advantage of me. Sincerely yours, Susan, from Texas, (with the southern drawl)."

I unrolled my sleeping bag and stretched out hands behind my head, looking up into the stains from the leaks due to monsoon rains. It hadn't dawned on me that I hadn't taken the time to eat. The thought didn't stop my eyes from closing and finding sleep. I thought about the warmth that was still present minus the itching. Ah, just before sliding into the slipstream of dreams.

The Indian Fair

After an uneventful shift, I logged myself out then took off outside under those ancient trees that lined Palace Avenue. Tourist traffic was heavier than the usual flow, and as I got closer to the square, I was slowed down by the sheer number of people that seemed to be in no hurry. In the square were hundreds of booths and every tribe seemed to be represented with their handiwork.

The sheer electricity stayed at a high pitch as the crowd bartered as people watched, happy to be spectators. Some were trying on bracelets, raising their arms to the sun to see how the light glistened designs on the silver. The Native people themselves were as much a part of the excitement as their varied and captivating wares. Some wore blue ribbons and others had red or green. Chubby English tourists stood out with their pale white skin and starched clothes with their hands behind their backs, sporting a noncommittal muted expression.

Spun Velvet

I stopped at a booth noticing a silver ring whose design I liked when a slender pretty Indian girl asked if she could help me. Right away, I sensed a chemistry between us begin to stir alive when I pointed to the ring and glanced into her eyes. She let there be just enough contact so I felt her silken skin as I took the ring from her, lingering against her hand as I did. I glanced at the ring keeping her face in my peripheral vision, watching her symmetrical features and white teeth instead of the ring, which I glanced back to, saying, "Very nice."

The awkward way she held her position told me what I wanted. She had courage in the face of my prying presence. Golly, her natural beauty was so pure and unassuming. Suddenly in this awkward moment, not really knowing what to say, I slid the ring slowly on and asked, "Can you make it any larger?"

Suddenly an older voice took over, and a larger and older-looking hand reached out to take the ring. "Here let me see it," the older lady's voice said with authority

I looked up into the eyes of what-must-have-been her mother as the chemistry of the moment then completely went south. Just like that, it abruptly ended as the crowd that pushed me to the next display of pottery.

Centrifugal forces

I found myself going with the overall momentum of the throng that moved counterclockwise around the booths—until a claustrophobia overtook me. I jumped to an inside group, going in the opposite direction, now thinking about that girl. Timing, it's all about the proper timing of a meeting so that the elements come together all at once in that randomness that it was really meant to be.

I stopped at a display of necklaces and rugs, and a lady glanced at me as if to say—*want to buy anything*? Her brown face had years of experiences of such churning events and knew the bottom line right away, projecting patience that said, *if you are interested you have all the time in the world*, as the crowd pushed its collective force around me standing there. I resisted and allowed them to part and go around me, as I reached down for a necklace and raised it up to the light so that the stones of amber, coral, shell, and turquoise glistened alive.

"How much?" I asked, setting the piece carefully back on the table.

"Twenty" was all she said, giving enough to say the price was final.

I had to smile at the difference between her and the girl before, as I pulled out a twenty and gave it to her. The transaction was made, she smiled and folded the bill, and I slid the necklace around my neck and fastened the catch.

Break in the Flow

Then the tide of the humanity surrounding the booths took over. I caught sight of the La Fonda Hotel in the corner of my eye and worked my way darting here then flowing with the current to where I could exit the throng and make it across the street. I headed to the restaurant that had Spanish music blaring out of a jukebox in the corner. I waited at the bar waiting as a bartender came over smiling.

"Nice necklace," the lady said, adding, "what can I get for you?"

"Pepsi on the rocks," I said, smiling at her expression of disbelief.

She tumbled ice into a glass then filled it all in a fluid motion subconsciously, so that she looked at me while she was busy. As the fizz came to the lip of the glass, she said, "Don't usually run into teetotalers during my shift," sliding the glass right in front of me—(an easy shuffleboard ten).

"I do my drinking when the magic's present, now I'm thirsty," I said, taking a deep drink, feeling the flavors run over my tongue.

"Your first time at Indian Market?" she said, wiping the counter.

"Yes, it's really something out there like I've never seen before. I'm from a little town in Colorado, and this is all new to me."

"People come here from all over the world to see the jewelry and feel the atmosphere of this place. I've been here two years and I've found out that people plan their vacation so they're here now."

Then a wave of customers came in and she was off mixing drinks. I finished my drink and left her a fifty-cent tip for her conversation, and headed toward the commune as the afternoon was waning. Further and further away from the square, it got quieter, and more normal rhythms prevailed as I went by alleys. Two sparrows were fighting over a crumb one had found. The larger one, of course, won out and flew off with its beak full.

I went past the capitol building and continued south, past the corner grocery store on Peralta and Santa Fe streets up a couple of blocks to that large wooden gate I knew by heart. Getting up at six and being on my feet eight hours, plus three more wandering around the jewelry booths, was catching up to me, so that by the time I got to the patio, I was barely making it.

CHAPTER 5

The Commune — a Breakdown

The meal was a great mix of broiled chicken and garden vegetables *ala* what Sue the Cook got free from friendly grocery stores nearby. Sue had the gift of improvisation in the kitchen second to no one. The evening meal was one thing I was looking forward to.

A few more crashers were on hand because of the Indian Market, so I got in line, and Sarah, who hardly spoke, dished the main course.

"Thanks," I said, forcing eye contact so that she had to smile, which was a big deal, since she wasn't one to show expression.

In some ways, I didn't understand the commune even one bit. I mean, it was nothing like the one I read about in *Look* Magazine; you know, where everybody was happy to be on his own groovy survival level with chicks that had kids on their hips cooking bowls of brown rice while the guys were in the fields sweating while they organically farmed. Then in the evening, everyone would be singing folks songs together; and for those who were single and had worked the fields all day, a curvaceous naïve blonde would come by with a second desert.

Nope, it wasn't that way—that reality is a bite was turning out true. Here, there were four people who seemed to control the operations, and each of them kept to themselves and were not approachable. They acted as if mingling with us crashers would affect them adversely in a *Ying-and-Yang*, out-of-control sort of way and throw them off, so that they'd have to consult the *I Ching* about what to do and toss the three pennies randomly the required six repetitions, then to translate it to the solid or broken lines of a hexagram, one on top of the other from top to bottom emphasizing accents—so that next the stack of six broke or solid lines would be looked up in the Book of Changes itself. The hexagram read out loud something like this—*The pheasant squawks in the field—a time for patient waiting*, it might say. Then each person's view of how that applied would ensue until everyone got pretty much off their chest what they were going to say anyhow, except now it was okay.

You can bet some were thinking, *huh, mind going over that again*, but no one wanted to give away they really had no clue, to give up their utter ignorance, so pretty much, it ran its course.

In a way, I was intrigued, at times the hexagram fit the occasion, and the description with the strategy would make sense. Since I was kicking in the twenties on a pretty regular basis, I was pretty much left alone to come and go as I wanted to, so one way or another, it didn't affect me much. In a way, I was that impartial observer and took note of how much credence they gave it, and went my way.

I was also beginning to catch on concerning the rules of the road. The core people who held the commune together were smart, as they used the word-of-mouth method to disseminate the rules—like how long you could stay on without kicking in real energy or substantial money, which everyone knew was for three days. Up to then, you could just crash and catch your breath freely. After that, you were expected to put in your hours helping out, or you were expected to move on, which most people did.

I was surprised to see how effective the rules worked out, since on the road, it is important to know you always have a place, and the importance of that one thing holds a lot of power—the power one does not want to screw with or lose at any cost. There seemed to be a one-week run for most transients, after which, the work got to them and they were on their way. That is, unless they had a talent or skill that was useful, such as Jason the carpenter or Sue the main kitchen boss.

Sue the Cook

Sue's talent lay in that she knew how to prepare food. Sue could come up with a gourmet delight out of the blue in a spontaneous way from meager contributions she'd find gathering discards from neighboring grocery stores. She had this staying power that everyone had to admit. When the pennies were tossed and the *I Ching* was consulted, it came out how the cook's power is the emperor's strength and something about how her order results from timeless patterns. Even if it would have come out in a negative way, she would have stayed since she was that important.

Her cooking became, by its nature, the life of the commune. The combinations of food, though the same, were never duplicated. There was always this added spice or that freshly created sauce that was truly first-class, which was always masked in subtleness. Her trick was pure magic. Somehow, she projected a controlled state of chaos in the kitchen as she went about cutting this or grating that, constantly in motion. Day after day, she'd still ended up putting it all in the same pot.

There was so much going on while she'd give orders to her help. She'd take this or that from spice bottles above the sink. You never knew how she knew how much went in each pot either, since she would never be caught measuring—it wasn't her style. Her sharp knife would slice through the gristliest meat around, only in the end, for it to be just the right touch to a thick soup. Her finished product was a work of art falling on your palate. She'd hover like all good artists do as we'd sample her product, licking our chops.

"Hmmmmm, pretty good," we'd say in unison. She'd wipe her hands on her apron, smile a second, and hum a country song, walking back to the kitchen with a wide grin on her face. She was the real center to the place as anything that her southern can-do spirit took on had to work.

They say in the Zen monasteries that the masters are the cooks. As I stayed on, I appreciated that saying more and more as the delicate touch she put on a meal became a constant. Good day or bad, in the back of my mind there would be some unique dish waiting for me, and that made each one of us feel that specialness in our day.

Her one drawback was that she enjoyed tasting her meals too, and though she had a pretty face with naturally curly blonde hair with skin so that deeply tanned with blue eyes that could match the clearest skies, she weighed in at about two hundred ten on a five-foot-two frame.

Ah, there was one other quality that was unique to her persona. Well, you didn't want her to get mad at you. If it was your turn to wash the dirty dishes or peel the potatoes, then you got your job done and done right. There were never any lists for you to know your turn. You were supposed to show up with the same enthusiasm to help, keeping in mind that she expected a job was to be done spot on. Everyone, I mean everyone, cut her as much slack as she needed.

I got along with her okay because I wasn't threatened by her, nor did I try to upstage her commitment or question her skill. I did my job and gave her the compliments that she deserved. She was always giving her all. Had she been, say a little shapelier, there might have been—well ah, some *could-of*s and big *maybe's* that I could feel between us in that electrical sort of way where really nothing got said verbally, but it was there by the way she would glance away.

But I held that in check, though I admit, I caught myself looking, knowing in her face there was a type of beauty, but I held back for there was a sincerity to her that I just wouldn't mess with, as I enjoyed her latest effort, glancing at the angles of her eyes and wondering what fifty pounds less would look like on her.

Kundalini for Sale

I was sitting beside Stan who had recently come in from Espanola. He was a slender guy with a wispy beard wearing a dye-cast tee shirt. "Yeah man, they got this yoga master up there, you won't believe," he said, savoring the moment of attention. "See, he offers to initiate the ladies for free, er well, that is, for a slight physical interaction." He added with a sarcastic tone, then elbowed me, "Too much huh? Hey, I'm thinking of taking up yoga seriously now myself."

Stan stood an easy six-foot-two without an ounce of fat. He had served in the Peace Corps in Honduras for a year. As a result, he had that worldly look about his outward demeanor, and with a wily smile and ready laugh he was a man for all seasons. He was a guy that gave you the vibe he could get out of any mess, while keeping that never-changing glint in his eye. I could have really used someone like him during my dark hours in max but that thought slid right on by.

I glanced over at Sue who was watching out of the kitchen window as she tossed and kneaded dough for the evening bread for tomorrow's breakfast.

"The yoga guy," Stan went on, "says the guy's power is to be shared and that it all comes from right here." He said pointing to his navel, "and that the female connects with that power like *yin and yang*. From that connection the singular power to procreate is derived."

His attempt to narrate the master's deal broke me up laughing. "No really," he interrupted, holding the moment to a serious level, only a split second later he was laughing right along beside me.

I had to admit, I liked Stan and would have liked to hang with him, but he was a wanderlust type and was gone the next day, which was what you learned about with this particular commune—that the people here did not want any personal tie, so you found yourself enjoying the moment and not extending it. That was both good and bad for me since that meant acceptance but without any meaning that time works into the interactions. What I was dying for inside was like a child needing a hug.

Some Bad News

Then the conversations around the table turned to a serious note about a rumor that this commune had been given public notice coming from the health department. The number of people housed at the residence was more than it was meant for, and by the end of September the place was going to close. The rumor spread as a troubled expression covered everyone's face, including Stan's, which really surprised me a great deal at the time.

"Huh, the commune is going to be closed," hushed voices repeated, hoping that anyone there would quickly repute any such silly notion but no one did. The atmosphere around the table became worse as a too-good-to-be-true look came to each person's countenance. Someone had come and had counted heads last week, and the health department had ruled that there were too many to insure health for the neighboring people, which translated simply they wanted us out.

The meal was silently eaten as each was shocked by this new reality. The reality we all thought we were somehow safe from with each other

Point of No Return

When Frank Lloyd tossed the pennies and the hexagram fell out, the saying went something like this, the chain has been broken, there is no recourse except to flee. This is time to plan a retreat. The words fell like stones in the silence to the deafness of disbelief. How could one day bring so much negativity without a warning?

Sue's face was the one that was the most broken up of all of them. I wandered by her and asked, "What will you do if it's really true?"

She glanced at me with a look of vacancy and wrung out her hands on her apron, "Oh, I…" but her words weren't ready to come. There was a pain in her voice, I held my breath and waited quietly. "Ah heck," she added with a smile, "the book should have read, good things don't last forever and I'd a would have then agreed, because that's what just happened, a good thing's over. What will you do, Cliff?" she asked with concern in her voice.

"I don't know," I said, thinking, *All I know is that I like it here.*

As she came closer, so that I could see old acne scars that I'd not noticed before, as well as the way her lips parted. She spoke in her true southern drawl, while she looked at me with her face close to mine so that I saw her irises clear blue glint that shown as she waited on me. We could have easily kissed, as I felt her breath on my cheek.

"I'll probably stay here since I love the free feel of this place," I said.

"Well, if you're ever in Atlanta look me up, Susan McCollough." We hugged each other and I felt a soft vibe warm like mercury.

Some Hidden Tears

Later that night, I woke up and had to go outside to the restroom, and while going past the open kitchen window, I heard muffled sounds, so I stopped just past the window and listened as my eyes adjusted. I saw the details of the darkness enough to see Sue as she was drying her eyes with one of the white kitchen towels. I continued to the restroom with that scene going in my mind

In so many ways, she was each of us in there crying her eyes out, having to leave the family we'd found around the breakfast table of oatmeal steaming up in bowls of white milk, sugar and raisins, or the occasional great cinnamon rolls that no one ever missed was the glue in our lives that quietly bonded us together. No one had thought about Sue's situation and how this new event could affect the master sergeant of the culinary arts negatively. No, and likewise, that was a stark statement about each of us and maybe why destiny was against this situation's continuation. Selfishness in and of itself will never have real staying power. *Thank you* was something that didn't get used that much the way *groovy man* and *outa sight* did on a regular basis. Sue deserved her own café in Atlanta more than this.

In the restroom I left ten napkins for the next guy on a ragged paperback of *Catcher in the Rye* on the brown wicker table beside the large tub. Even the dripping sink and the cracked mirror had memories woven with them. The crack ran in a jagged way from left to jutty right, going up—a remnant of Stanley the Peddler's bad acid trip. He had stayed long enough to sell his Florida key chains that had either a plastic swordfish or an orange starfish.

Yes, going by the kitchen window, it was more about Sue and how life pulled you on to a greater use of your talents than it was about any of the rest of us vagabond travelers.

Time Slides On

As August slid by into September, the nights were getting colder and the numbers quietly thinned one at a time as they left, and the chill in the evening reminded each of us winter wasn't far off as the heater in the corner looked smaller and smaller with each new night. The incense and the fantasies of summer dissolve into September towards the final closing date, and only the diehards complained loudly as that date came closer, but they knew it was inevitable and soon they too were gone.

For me, I knew what I was going to do, I had made that decision back in Boulder in that library leafing through *Look* magazine. I was now hooked on the pale blue sky and the free-flowing square where time went easy, passing with the coming and going of people, all of whom were in their own way completely a thing of wonder with Aspen Peak in the background, as well as Santa Fe Mountain distant and deep with dark blue of spruce and pine standing high, majestic. Yes, and there was no way I would ever be leaving this.

CHAPTER 6

A Week to Stay on

The notice was tacked on, stating that we all had one more week. This Thursday night got cold, as I shivered away in my bag. At the first crack of light through the telephone wires, I glanced at the heater going full bore. It looked even smaller, so I started off to the hospital where I could change and shower. The hot water brought life to my goose-bumped body. With my bones thawed, my attitude was ready for this day.

The ER started out pretty slow with just regular stuff, a day verging on boredom so you almost wished that something would happen to break the monotony, but you never wished specifically that somebody would get hurt. There's something thrilling about the chaos of an emergency room when within it all, you can feel the battles for life are raging full.

Little Andrea

I glanced at Lucy and pointed to my watch as if to say *break time*, so I left walking over the shiny tile floor toward the snack bar. When I got back, they had wheeled a little girl in with an injured leg. She had been part of the Zozobra festivities parade sitting on a float. She had been relaxing on the back side of a flatbed semitrailer with her leg dangling over the edge as the driver had been backing up, going around a telephone pole, and he'd almost made it—that was until the pole caught her leg and pinched it tighter until her scream shut everything down in a big shocked hurry.

But the damage had been done and muscle pulled away, so that you could see the leg bones midst the clotted blood. Luckily, there is an automatic numbing that our body kicks in, and that process was in full effect when I came on the scene. My job was to clean out the wound the best way that I could so the doctors could get to see the extent of the damage done.

The girl kept asking me if she could get a better look at the gash, but sometimes the vision of such a horrendous abrasion could easily make her go into shock at the mere sight of it.

"Ah, don't worry about it, you'll be okay," I said, reassuring her, being careful to keep my tone casual to belie the seriousness of the injury. I could overhear the doctors who were talking behind my back, mentioning the possibility of amputation as they conferred.

I dabbed the four-by-four gauze pads over and in the grooves that the torn-away flesh made, being sure to be gentle. After they finally all agreed that they would need to see X-rays before their decision, and I was sent upstairs with the little girl on the gurney to get them.

"Why can't I look?" she asked.

"Won't do any good anyhow," I answered matter-of-factly.

The dialogue went as the elevator chimed its way up the floors. All in all, it took about twenty minutes to get the pictures shot since there had to be certain positions with her leg just so. Before I could get in there to help, she would yell out, "Ooow."

With X-rays done, I couldn't help but admire her raw courage. On the way down, I said a silent prayer. It was sincere, the kind you don't usually say, which you put your whole heart in. I had just completed when the elevator door opened to the hall that lead to the ER. When I got back, her mom and dad were waiting for her. The mother took one look at the leg and gasped then turned pale almost fainting. The little girl quickly caught on, crying out, "It hurts, Mommy."

I quickly said, "Mommies worry too much about their children, especially when they are hurt," and I wheeled her into the room, gave the doctors the X-rays, and asked to see the parents outside. "You've got to help me," I said, looking directly into their eyes. "I'm trying to keep her positive and you've got to help," I added intensely, noticing a nurse just beyond them with a clipboard in her hand.

"Maybe," the father said, looking at his wife, "we should stay here."

When I got back, the doctors had decided there was a good chance with surgery the leg could be saved, so I wheeled her past her parents and giving them a thumbs-up, and back into the elevator we went, only this time it was positive.

"What's your name?" I asked, looking down at her deep brown eyes.

"Andrea," she answered, biting on her lower lip to ease the pain.

"Well, Andrea, don't worry cause they're going to fix you all up." We had eye contact—hers to my truth index—I passed, as a smile came to her face.

When the doors closed and the surgical tech took the gurney, a deep exhaustion swept over me. As I turned to the elevator, my hands were shaking as I pushed the bottom floor button and the elevator started down, clinging as each floor passed by. That night on the way back to the commune, the moon was full and I felt this inner glow—even as tired as I was, trudging back finally through that large wooded gate with the ornate hinges. I went by the kitchen, and Sue was there putting away the pots.

I glanced in, and we made eye contact and we both smiled. "How'd it go?" she asked sensing weariness in my body language.

"A little girl got hurt today in the parade and I kept her spirits up." I answered, going over the still-fresh memory of her. "I kept her from falling into that hole that keeps going down," I said, walking into the kitchen.

Sue nodded, listening across the table. I sat down and put my head on my hands and sighed. She extended her hand across the table toward me and took mine. "You know, we make a great team, with our never-say-die attitudes." There was in her voice an opening for me to make that connection.

I smiled, "You're right," feeling a suppleness in her soft clasp. But I was spent, too emotionally extended—the window closed.

She pulled her hand back, "That little girl was very lucky tonight."

"Thanks," I said, reaching for her hand and squeezing it firmly.

"I'm going to miss you," I said, and I meant it more than I knew.

"This place was a one-in-a-million shot, I'm glad it was our time," she said, getting up and going to the last dirty dishes in the sink.

I smiled and turned to the door, "You're sounding like that book, only that you didn't toss the pennies."

"Good night," she said smiling, as I walked out into the night air.

Last Night at the Commune

40

My eyes adjusted quickly to the sparse light out in the cool air, and I found the door to the sleeping quarters and went inside. There were only four other sleepers in sleeping bags, and it wasn't long before I too was nestled inside, glancing up at designs from the leaky roof and the past monsoon rains.

The vision of that jagged wound in Andrea's leg kept coming back. It really was much worse than anything I had ever seen in the ER, and how that little girl managed the pain that must have been—remembering that she bit her lower lip and how she kept glancing back at me for my reaction to the mess, which I had to block out and make out that it was just a little cut. I could tell that there was plenty of pressure on me right then. I was proud of myself that I hadn't buckled—that I had hung in there. All the emotional twists had left me now with a shot of adrenaline that would not let sleep come, even though I was beat, so I decided that the best thing for me would be to take a shower.

I made my way over and around four scattered bodies past the kitchen window, the picnic tables, the wind chimes that were tinkling out a melody, compliments of the breeze. I stopped there and thought about the good times, as a filmy set of scenarios stood out and played their dynamics. It could have gone on forever that way, missing them.

As the cool breeze with a strong hint of autumn made me shiver, I turned to the bathroom and opened the door. A steamy hot cloud met me as I took a step inside and stopped—movement from the shower curtains seemed to beckon me.

"Excuse me," I said, letting them know who the intruder was. I hesitated, not quite sure what to do as my heart kicked in, and I saw her hand come around the curtain beckoning, so I reached out and took hold of the edge of the plastic divider.

41

"Oh, Cliff," she said, holding her arms to cover her bare breasts, and since I had already committed my presence to her space, I awkwardly stood there with me holding my place.

She glanced into my eyes, and saw what I had thought was okay. "No, Cliff, that part of this southern belle stays pure," she said.

I retreated, embarrassed, I had read the situation so badly. I went back to my sleeping bag, and promptly went to sleep. The next morning on my bag was a note with a flower over it. "Dear Cliff," it read, "I must say that I had thought of us like that. Going to miss you. I left early, since I found a last-minute ride. Sincerely yours, Sue." I smiled while I read it and then I took off on my shoe-leather commute to work.

CHAPTER 7

Life Moves On

By the time my shift ended, I was tired when I wandered around to see the head nurse about a matter she wanted to talk with me about. I thought nothing of it as I waited until her door opened and that nurse I had seen when I had lectured Andrea's parents about leaving me alone to work with Andrea.

She cleared her throat in a business way and began, "Mr. Alexander." In my mind I already knew this was not going to be good news. I had that knife-in-the-back feeling I had received from that icy glance that other nurse gave me as she slipped out the door. She continued, "There seems to be a problem that I must address. One of our nurses overheard you address the parents of one of our patients in the hallway, and I've got to tell you that we just can't have our employees address the parents of our patients in such a rude and uncaring manner." Her voice rose adding, "We just can't tolerate such behavior in our employees."

I held my breath and had a good idea what was coming next, and even though as she said the words, it was as if she was talking to a person next to me. "I have no choice but to let you go. This will be your last shift at this hospital."

As I cleaned out my locker, there was a certain numbness to my thinking that made everything like it was a blur of successive actions that I saw myself going through that followed me like a cloud as I left the shiny floors for the last time.

A monsoon rainstorm had moved in. I wandered around the square and the shops that fronted it, trying to get inner momentum going, to break up my fear that I might not be able to find a place to crash. The numbness eased in a wave of thoughts about my next challenge—that of getting a place to crash.

The funny thing about Santa Fe is that it's at seven thousand feet, which means the weather shifts can go to extremes in a hurry and the temperature can drop twenty degrees with no warning. Such was the lesson that I was learning first-person present tense, but I was determined that Santa Fe was going to be my destiny and that meant there would be a place for me. As the evening turned into twilight, the rains ebbed and flowed. I continued and hooked around Park Avenue toward Catron Street. By now the rain was dripping down my back and I was really cold.

The Indian Pad

I was on the verge of giving up and heading for the Hotel Santa Fe, where you could get a bed in an open dorm setup for five bucks, when I saw young people who were coming out of a place.

"You looking for a party?" one of them asked me out of the blue.

"Yes, and a place to crash would be fine right now," I answered.

They laughed at my honesty and said, "Hey, what's your name?"

"Cliff," I chimed in, following them as they retraced their steps.

One of them went to a door and opened it without any hint of hesitation, then went in and looked around, "Here's Cliff," he interrupted as about ten people who were talking to one another stopped and looked up at me with my hair streaming down my forehead.

There was an awkward hesitation as they searched my features and could easily make out that I was the only pale face there.

"He's cold and he's looking for a place to crash. What'a you say?" he asked.

One of them chimed in, "Your last name wouldn't be Custer?" At which they all laughed and watched me shake my head no. "Well, then," one of them said, "Come on in and get a Budweiser." He motioned me with his hand to follow him and so I did. He was tall and slender and had a herk-jerky way of moving. As I followed him, I took my pack off to release some weight.

We went into the kitchen with its white tile floor and tan walls. I set my pack by the refrigerator to which he nodded okay. He handed me a Budweiser, which I opened and followed him into the living room, where a *Who* album was playing softly. Conversations were going on in all directions, oblivious to me. Indians aren't big on making the first move so I just sat there acting as natural as I could, just plain glad to be out of the rain. That night I slept nearest to the door in the least-best place.

A Temporary Fix

The next day I went and got bread and hung out with them, trying my best to fit in and to make friends. The guy that originally broke the ice for me was called Buffy Shanta. He had a slender build with high cheek bones and a straight face. He could tell you a joke and have you in stitches and not even smile.

There was this us-against-the-world mentality about the group that I identified with right off, and even if I was white, my heart wasn't. He and I ended up being the ones who made the beer runs at night. He knew all the short-cut alleyways, had a good sense of direction so that even in the pitch-black moonless night, we'd come out right behind or across the street from any certain liquor store without fail.

Dogs, for some reason, also cut us this swath when I was with Buffy. He was a Mescalero Apache, and they could sense with him there was this finality that said, mess with me end up dead, that even dogs picked up in a hurry, which he would joke about. I saw that there was this quiet energy underneath him that told you to be careful about pushing him to any degree. But for some reason, we hit it right off, relating with simple things that we both saw in our own way where there was humor, like the way one dog would immediately go subservient to another. He'd chime in a dialogue saying, "Please don't kick my butt," with his impeccable timing, and we'd both bend over from laughing.

It was easy to see that we liked each other but he was still Mescalero, and they are not known for an overabundance of facial expression, which was an overstatement that his blank look would play out.

Then there was Penguin, a short person from the Aleutian Islands who was a good artist and had a gallery over off of San Francisco right west of Walgreens and across the street, then up the stairs. We both liked Tracey, younger sister of Sarah (Buffy's girlfriend). She had a slender athletic body with high cheek bones and good skin. She was from the Nambe Pueblo and was staying with the group. We both tried to hustle her but neither of us had any luck at all.

I settled in and fit best I could as the situations came up. Dinner was a matter of going over to the Safeway Store on Catron. Sarah's raincoat held a full chicken as she bought a pack of gum. Pulling it off with quiet dignity was easy since they had been conquered after all and were only beginning to get even with what they'd lost. Generations before had instilled in them a strong sense of survival. To them it was simple, when you got hungry you went and found; you owed nothing to the white man and less to his fancy stores.

The determination I saw on their countenances just astounded me. Humor later came with their own version of what just took place that rolled out with their in-depth descriptions of the clerk's faces on our way back to the pad as we laughed. After we ate what our stealthy endeavors had yielded, we'd sit back with a full stomach and throw a rolled-up sock back and forth trying to fake out the person who wasn't quite ready to receive it. As the night got thicker with its black, we'd fall one by one off to those dreams that we each silently rode our one true steed, not knowing what tomorrow might bring nor for that matter caring since we, in a strange way that I did not understand, had each other.

However, I for one, was not used to not having money of my own, so I decided to go and find myself a job.

Dishwasher Wanted

The next day I headed out on Cerrillos Road, ready to find a job. There was a certainty to my step, a determination in my stride right past the Indian School and the motels and pawn shops past The Pantry Restaurant "Help Wanted" sign in its window. I filled out the application and immediately got interviewed by the owner whose last name turned out to be Alexander.

"A dollar thirty-five per hour is what the dishwasher job pays, and right now we only need help two days a week part time, so that means, you would get about eighteen dollars per week." He added, wiping gray hair off his forehead.

Right away it seemed like it was the perfect job for me to handle with plenty of free time and just enough pressure to be a challenge, so with a smile from both of us we shook hands and it was done. Afterward I celebrated getting a Dr Pepper at this burger stand that was just past the Indian School campus going toward the city. At the juke box I picked out a Junior Walker song. *What does it take to win your love*, words enveloped the place and my mind along with the flavors of the Dr Pepper I was sipping.

The job had allowed me this release from the unknown of need, and I glanced over at the occupants and saw an Indian girl eyeing me. She had the wide cheekbones of a Sioux and a free way about her and the way she used her hands communicating with the guy with her. I could tell the chemistry was mixing between us as they left and headed back toward the direction of the school.

I turned to the music that was going into a saxophone solo in which Junior really starts to wail and string out the notes thin and tight and then back into the rhythm at the last movement. That girl came back in with a girlfriend with her and sat down. I spent five minutes trying to find a line to hook up but no luck. The intense attraction I felt was too much for me to overcome, so I did the next best thing—I left as cool as I could.

Outside heading north on Cerrillos, I went by a KFC restaurant and continued alongside the cemetery where this dog came out as I walked, the image of her face came to my mind clearly along with this vibe that there was this thread woven between us. The dog started barking like I was going to dig up one of the graves. The wrought-iron fence was between us, and his owner came out to see what the commotion was and smiled at me as I waved back.

Back at the pad, things were changing with the group dynamics as some sisters had moved in and didn't like the idea of my presence and how this white guy could be crashing when he was really the enemy, so that morning when I had gotten up late and found myself alone, Angeline came in with a stern face.

"Alexander, you've been here for more than two weeks now, right? You know that this isn't the only place in town for you to crash in?" she added.

Buffy wasn't around to back me up here, and now she was on a roll, holding all of the cards since I hadn't chipped in any rent money. She was looking out the window at the leaves' slight yellow hue.

"Well," I said, "I'll load up my stuff and be going right away then," though I wanted to add that she was a jerk. Ending and beginning was becoming this theme I had fallen into, so I headed with my knapsack on my back into the clear blue day.

Finding a Place

I headed west of town toward the barrio part where rent was cheap, following Guadalupe til I hit Paseo de Peralta, and I kept on walking, keeping my eyes primed for any For Rent signs. I headed west past an elementary school with the kids out playing. I crossed the street and started past an adobe house with a porch and, sure enough, there was that For Rent sign in the front window. I walked up and knocked on the door, hoping for the best.

This lady with silver gray hair that was pulled back into a ponytail answered the door, looking at me for a long hesitant split-second.

"I'm wondering about the room," I said, looking at her blue eyes.

"Yes, we have a place. It's out back," she said, pointing to the back, adding, "and I do the cooking ,and you'd be welcome to come by," in a southern drawl that was more midwestern, in her blue dress that had a flower print to it. I followed her to the side of the house where an old garage had been converted into a cheap apartment.

"It rents for sixty a month," she said, putting her hands on her hips. For sixty dollars a month, I couldn't have asked for a better place. I was overjoyed at my luck, since it wasn't that far at all from town.

New Digs

It wasn't long before my new neighbors made themselves known. They were the boarders from the main house to the east. Let's see, of course, there was Elizabeth with her slender body and hair in a bun or tightly pulled ponytail. Later, I found out she had split from Bible Belt parents in Kansas and had hitchhiked until she ran out of money and confidence whereupon she committed herself to the mental hospital at Las Vegas.

Then there was chubby Elena with dark eyes and ready smile who would rock on the balls of her feet while she stood still bouncing her overweight body that juggled much like jelly while she talked. And there was chain-smoking-for-all-you're-worth Jessie—a slightly built black lady, who'd sit alone on the wicker chair on the back porch and smoke a cigarette she had just rolled with the paper in her mouth with panting breaths. She'd sit by the hour looking into the distance at nothing really. Later, I found out that they were all releases from the mental ward "*Ruled harmless*" by the state and allowed to live out in society.

My first week there I had left a large jar of peanut butter out on the top of my dresser, only to come home to find it cleaned out, left on the counter. They had proudly washed so well that it had sparkled shiny. I was pissed, though I had to smile, then I got a real stern look. "Next time," I said, looking at them in the doorway of the garage, "I'll lodge an official complaint to the hospital, so if you don't want to go back, you'd better stay out of here." They left my place mumbling and downcast walking back to the house. They never did repeat their breaking-and-entering ways.

CHAPTER 8

Catching Currents

I was now really on my own with very few expectations other than showing up to do the dishes and paying the rent. But without people around me, boredom slowly set in, and that brought me into the Canyon Bar that I'd heard about from the other fulltime dishwasher. It was an adobe building right off the sidewalk of Canyon Road. I walked in and passed the bar with the variety of half-full liquor bottles from all over the world lined up just in front of the customary mirror.

In the back there was a larger room with scattered worn green-felt tables and a hallway opposite, that lead into a larger area that was used for dancing that had a raised stage where a band could set up to play. In the room with the tables, there was a group around one table. I timidly walked over and pulled up a chair nearby to eavesdrop. The way they all sat around so relaxed, they had to be friends, as I picked up on what was an ongoing discussion.

"Life is full of chasing rainbows," a man with a red beard said. He had a thick scalp of orange red hair with freckles on his face

"Okay," another man countered, "I'll agree with that but I'll add, that making love along the way helps out a great deal as you go." With that he leaned back and accepted the laughter of the group as if he were a high-wire performer who had completed a feat.

Immediately, I was taken in by this off-the-wall group of men. Later, I found out that the red-haired guy's name was Clyde. "With lots of skeletons in my closet," he said in the same breath. The other man, Norm Moser, was a Beat poet who had migrated from "The Bay" and came here to get away. Norm's way with words made him adept as a perfect foil for Clyde who turned out to be a painter of landscapes around the town.

Norm would compose as he went along with the ride. At times, he seemed to be just as surprised with what he'd come up with, and he'd get this look on his face, which would change into a smile, and the smile would disappear and a focused look would follow. I pulled up my chair to get a closer look—a won-over fan already. The argument was a classic match between left and right brains.

"Procreation at any time has its own special set of rewards," Clyde parried back, adding the remark, "Check."

Everyone waited on Norm's comeback. The barmaid came by, saying, "Time out," as if she was ready to take orders, adding, "You look thirsty, who's ready for another round?" She had blonde hair cut short and a loose way of moving so that she seemed to be in complete state of relaxation. She seemed to know who all had said yes, as she moved on only then to come back with what everyone was drinking on her tray.

Norm kissed his thumb and forefinger in a French sort of way and said, "Ah ha," and gently patted her cheek as she went by. "Thank you, my dear," Norm had said, "Likewise," she rebutted. The table went, "Ahhhhh," in response and we all laughed.

Norm stroked his mustache that made him look like a watchmaker. "Let me see, very interesting," he said as if playing a chess match and as if he'd come up with just the right move as he leaned back and said, "Clyde, you got to admit rainbows don't keep you warm in the middle of the night. Admit it, you either love it or you don't." With that said, he took a big swig of his beer and smiled, and he replaced the empty glass as if he'd just moved his queen.

"So, you're saying that you don't believe in rainbows," Clyde probed.

"No, I'm saying that I'd rather have Kate right here any time," he said, reaching out as the barmaid had just turned behind him to fill another order as he wrapped his arms around her small waist stopping her progress.

"Objection," Clyde said, "illegal use of the establishment's property." Everyone laughed, already drawn into the friendly give and take

"No offense to either of you but I'm going home by myself tonight, but thank you for the invitation," she said, unwrapping Norn's arms and giving the table a salute, going back filling orders.

"You can't blame a guy for trying," Norm said with a smile, "since we were talking about rainbows, I couldn't help myself."

Kate looked back to the table and broke into a laugh herself. She then filled her tray with ten drinks and balanced it as she wove between tables and around patrons. The whole table was caught up by the finesse of her fluid motion, as if she were a ballet dancer. She'd come to the next obstacle, size it up balancing the platter; just prior to contact, she'd slide by in counter direction, keeping the drinks safe on their tittering tray as if she was on a tightrope. As if for that moment, she could've been part of a circus act, so that spontaneously they all applauded, as I joined in.

"A work of art," Norm said, as he took a sip of his frothy drink. "Truly, love is wasted on the young like they say," he muttered. "It's taken all this time to figure them out and now."

Clyde interrupted, "That now it's all just too late to do any good."

"Clyde," Norm added, "you're a poet trapped in a painter's body."

With that, a somber mood enveloped the table as each fell silent, and they got a deeper look in their eyes as they sipped their drinks. I got that feeling that the caged animal was prowling so I stretched and felt like introducing myself but thought against it. Glancing to my right, I could see into that adjacent larger room.

Music in the Air

In the dim light I could make out that a band was setting up, so I wandered with my drink in hand, and sat at an empty table. Musicians were hooking up and tuning their instruments. I watched as they got ready, each in sync with the other. As they got closer to being ready, they got their game faces on. One, a tall skinny guy with long thin blonde hair had his banjo out and was picking out random tunes, taping his foot as the drummer picked up the beat with him. They were giving each other eye contact, bobbing their heads as the beat became more apparent. The other guy came in with a violin, which seemed an odd combination—until the violin went to work between the banjo riffs and added a lively up-and-down rollercoaster feel to the music.

The tall guy seemed to be the leader as they all waited on him, playing easy at first like kids getting used to the feel of the water. He stepped up to the mike, adjusted it, and cleared his throat. "We'd like to play a ditty we've been working on," he said, adding, "We like to call it Carol's things." Then they took off with the violin filling the gaps the banjo left and hung on the transitions that could go either way as the banjo came back in unexpectedly.

54

The music went around the narrative of Carol's world of pursuit, with the drummer in the background *kerthump, kerthump* keeping time. The words ran about scenarios of Carol and her many pretty things. Words and music spread through the darkened room like magic.

I leaned back with her picture the song wove in my mind, as if I had just met her with my foot taping under the table along with everyone else. When the song ended, there was a three- second pause as we sat in the darkness of the room and savored the moment. Then scattered applause erupted with volume.

"Thank you, thank you very much," the lead banjo player said. "By the way," he added, "I'm Sammy, that's Lou on the violin, and over there beating the skins is Little Eddy." Eddy smiled and did a *ratta tat tat*. "Eddy likes to ham it up," he interjected. "Now we've got some bluegrass you might like."

They broke into a bluegrass song that had blues to it as well, which the violin player pulled off by holding a single note longer, and off that note he'd go and hold on to the next note too, which in turn, made the drummer go into a steady downbeat that the banjo player would, as if he was a lead guitar player, go into this lead riff at the same time, and then fade back out. So it went song to song as the rhythms greased the minutes and time got relative the way time does when there's magic present.

"Our last one is one we're still working on, so be patient," he said, looking at the drummer for the downbeat, again nodding his head. He looked back out and said into the mike, "It's called changing," as the banjo ripped its rhythms and chords with the beat, the violin guy put his violin down and reached for a bagpipe and at a part when the melody caught hold he came in steady holding this note with such intensity so you held your breath the way the guys played with so much feeling, that it pulled you in. There were no words just notes with an intense riveting beat and that wailing bagpipe that kept a steady underlying melody.

Suddenly from one of the tables, a man's voice came in a deep tone. It was low and long as he chanted to the melody keeping the pitch. I felt a similar urge to jump in but was too embarrassed to join in. When another man joined the first one singing deeply from his gut, it was too much for me to hold back, so that even if I was going to make a fool of myself, I joined in and could feel part of myself going to this emotional edge of where I really had never been before—going with the bagpipe, which seem to pull something out of me. I wanted to match the tunes that wailed with the music of that trio. In that dark bar room, a Canyon Bar Choir sang out with their souls up into the dark night since the walls could not hold the drive to mix with that melody that for that one second that bar was full of life's harmony. Just like that, it was over and the closing sign went on.

We left, each one wanting to stay and be part of one more song, feeling as we hit the night air that winter was not far off. The night absorbed us as we got in cars or headed down the street back to our singular existences; but now reinforced with our soaring maybe how eagles feel once they have found those jet streams.

I, for one, walked with this warm glow, for I had found a place, a place where I felt I belonged and, as I walked, I felt like shouting.

CHAPTER 9

Letting Life Find Me

It was a day off from the dishes—get up easy, around ten o'clock, lay around and watch light play off the ceiling, running shadows that were in sync with the bush rustling outside on the window as the breeze from the mountain ran through the Santa Fe streets.

Nothing was on my mind except to get out and go exploring. Going out on Paseo de Peralta across Cerrillos, I went to a corner grocery store with windows covered in wrought-iron, fancy twirling designs, saying that after-hours the store wasn't safe. I went in with the buzz of flies that circled the fresh fruit stand over worn floors that had witnessed miles of people browsing, children finding where the stuff was stored, running errands. The tons of weight over the years the tile had cumulatively borne.

I got a bag of Fritos and a cool Pepsi and headed to the counter where an older lady with gnarled fingers manned the register. She smiled weakly after I laid my items out in front of her. I gave her two dollars, and she counted my change and bagged the stuff, which I took and left finding where I could sit down and eat.

I watched the scenery made of people and traffic going on by. I glanced around at the simple architecture of the nearby houses that were light brown stucco with tiny front yards and chain-link fences to keep out dogs and keep the children safe. Some had potted plants hanging from archways with flowers growing over edges and into the open spaces.

I finished the bag of Fritos and the last swig of Pepsi and headed going north on Cerrillos, taking my time, as women sang hanging their wash. I picked up snatches of a Spanish melody riding an expressive voice. I was feeling part of the essentialness of this old town that dated back to Conquistadores that brought the priests, so the oldest buildings are Catholic churches.

At Alameda I went right and headed toward the mountain that rose in the distance, dark blue with its slopes full of spruce and pine, fed and watered from the deep winter snows. As I walked up the street toward town, the mountain loomed larger. I was free on this day to let the flow take its course for me to find out what discoveries were to make in this day, clear blue and bright.

A young women's voice sparkled with emotion in the song she sang. It was a Spanish song whose words I couldn't make out, though I tried, and whose melody was captivating in its simple beauty and fluidity. I slowed down more, so I could listen better to what she was saying. I could just see her on the other side of a driveway in the backyard, hanging clothes as she bent down to unravel another shirt. She was shapely and had high cheek bones; the symmetrical balance to her face came together as my view caught sight of this scene of both beauty and harmony. She had on a white blouse that contoured well to her endowments. Mid-motion she straightened out, arched her back, then looked around catching me pretty much invading her privacy with my staring look. A quick smile came to her lips and she turned back to the laundry. She shyly glanced back and smiled again.

I said, "*Buenos días*," in my best Spanish my high school teacher would've been proud of. She hung up the shirt, glanced back and said, "*Buenos días*." I tried to seem as natural and as unhurried as I could standing there, while I took in beauty, style, and naiveté of expression all at once. "Is this the way to town?" I asked, trying to fill in the awkwardness.

She got a blank look on her face and said, "*No hablo inglés.*"

My mind was clicking off all the possible options but came up cold since my Spanish was limited, as were my chances of hooking up. *Crap*, I couldn't help but think, and the moment slid by and she went back to work, singing that song she had been before.

Then just like that, I was back to my midmorning walk all by myself as I continued up the street with the impression she had left still on my mind. It had been a case of so close and yet so far away all in one.

I walked on under the blue turquoise of the sky that spread out and thought about that magic she had woven with her beauty, and about how women have that natural quality about their presence. They know they have it, no matter what they happen to be doing as with her hanging up today's laundry, singing in her usual way that she'd probably had been doing since she was a little girl. There was a confidence to her song—a pureness of expression, a no-holding-back, as much a part of her beauty as her looks.

My mind dissected the moments and the content as I walked and could see the tops of the buildings of Santa Fe. I kept on my way, allowing that lucky encounter to dissolve back, thinking, *okay, so I should've paid better attention to my Spanish teacher and maybe I would have been able to have made more of that moment. But you can't win them all*, I countered in my mind.

Mid-morning Sustenance

And so, I headed over the dusty streets with the barking dogs with still more ladies hanging up their wash, singing as they did. I wandered up the streets to where people were more numerous as they came and went into the different stores along the street. I wandered up to Walgreens and walked up to the lunch counter. A blonde girl, wearing granny glasses came over to take my order, with peering sensitive blue eyes.

"I'll have toast and a milk," I said to her expectant glance.

"You got it," she said, scribbling on her pad.

I looked at the mirror on the wall that lined the whole length of the opposite side of the diner. I smiled to check my appearance with my broken front tooth. I had a dentist take off the cap had masked the gap after wrestling a kid in fourth-grade summer school. I was tired of being afraid of how I'd look with it off, and I was adamant to free myself, hoping that facing one fear just might help me face them all. My theory had failed miserably, except in one sense I was free, except not now as I glanced at what people saw when I spoke.

She came back and slid the plate with the toast in front of me. I opened one of the jelly containers and spread it evenly, and for five minutes my taste bud mixed milk with jellied bread allowed associations climb through the years like a hot knife sliding through butter, childhood snatches alive, how flavors can unleash the best memory spontaneously. I finished the toast and milk and left two dollars for the waitress, which would have covered it, and waited for my change as she came back and looked part way into my eyes and turned.

Walking out of Walgreens, I couldn't help but feel the life pulsing since Santa Fe kicks in at ten o'clock when the caffeine takes effect, give or take ten minutes. The Indians over on the square to sell their stuff under the roof in front of the Governor's Palace, ready for the ten o'clock hour. They start laying it out around eight-thirty. I wandered over, taking my time to check out the unique displays laid out on blankets. One Indian that seemed to be the overseer of the whole displays came over, "How are you doing?" he said, offering me pinon nuts.

I took some, saying, "Not too bad, I'm checking out the jewelry." Putting one nut in my mouth with the intent to crack the shell without crushing the inside softer meat that had a nutty flavor. I pulled out of my mouth a crunched-up mass of shells and nut that I spit into my hand. The Indian ladies who manned their displays all seemed to notice. They seemed to be "still life's" sitting behind their jewelry rows, smiling at me and looking at each other, smiling more.

I hadn't got paid yet from the Pantry Restaurant so I nodded no, "Can't buy anything now, I haven't got paid yet." In the back of my mind I was looking for that winnowy Indian girl I had bumped into during the Indian Fair looking at that ring. But no such luck today, as I finished up the line of displays.

Then I headed over to the square where there was motion all over, as the eternal orange Frisbee sailed back and forth between hippies with shirtless underfed bodies wearing beads. There was a rhythm to the square as if a conductor had control over the people, trees swaying, animals, cars cruising that flowed in their own ways, some coming in contact, some nearly so, some avoiding this place where motions captured the eye. The dynamics stayed on the surface by the manner in which two would walk together. You could read the body language of lovers or of friends or of acquaintances by perceiving the distances or the relaxation or stress in the touch, how the accidental coming together allows one to formulate all the rest.

I leaned back and let the warmth from the sun find my arms and face, feeling the breeze cool me at the same time as the scene played on around me.

To the Library

Feeling the need to write, I went across the street to the library, which was just north from the east corner of the Governor's Palace. I hit the entrance and went inside and up the brick steps. On the bulletin board I noticed an ad for a concert, this coming Sunday evening at the Governor's Palace. I made a mental note and continued past the main counter where I gathered up *People*, *Field and Stream*, and *The New Yorker*. I was ready to settle in, once I found a seat at the main table.

Crazy Lucero

I was getting into a *New Yorker* cartoon from a dog's point of view who went by a restroom with a fire hydrant on the door. It showed the owner shaking his head like he couldn't follow him in. I was beginning to catch the humor when a Spanish guy came in and sat down right beside me with a cowboy hat on, with dirty hands, a large mustache, a ruddy complexion that said he'd been outside for most of his life, reminding me a lot of the guy that picked me up back on Pecos Trail.

"Sons of bitches," he said just loud enough so that I easily heard him. I was still glancing at the cartoon and trying not to let him interrupt. He took a deep breath, obvious that something had set him off. In my peripheral vision, I could see a deep furrow on his forehead, so I glanced up from my cartoon and let him into my field of vision.

He looked at me and said, "They'll take your blood too." Adding, "those taxmen are worse than vultures, *aye caramba*," he injected. "I mean, like blood-suck leeches. *Madre mía*," he said a little louder, making the sign of the cross.

It was almost comical but he was serious so I held my smile. I sensed a hint of sensitivity in his eyes as he shot me a deeper look, and I could see he was sizing me up to see how I was responding. I glanced at a bull fight mural right behind him on the wall, noticing the paradox of tights on a macho matador with the bull stampeding toward him with his horns down ready to rip and tear.

"I don't know who I dislike the most," he went on in a half whisper as people around us were already giving us those cold hard stares. I waited for him to continue, drifting back to the matador poster.

"It's about the land. It becomes part of you in here," he added, pushing his hand hard against his chest in the area near his heart. I thought of Dad's ranch in Paonia, Colorado, and knew he was right, which if he hadn't of sold it was where I would be right now. "The land is like a woman," he went on, "she'll give and give, but you've got to take care of her, treat her with real respect." He stopped and looked out the window touching his moustache. "Oh, my name is Edward Lucero. I haven't seen you around here."

"I'm new. I hitchhiked here in August. My name's Cliff Alexander." We shook hands and I could feel he had the grip of a ranch hand as we felt each other's power through our hands and then let go.

He leaned back in the chair and put his hands behind his neck. "I like you," he said, "you remind me of myself, or the way I was, a long time ago," he added and smiled at a personal thought. "Land is like my blood, but my kids can only think about money, they don't care," he said sighing with a forlorn look on his face. "I don't know who is worse—the taxmen or my kids right now." He then looked around and spit in his hand for effect. He glanced out of the window as something had caught his eye that he could focus on to deflect the pain he was feeling inside.

I felt like hugging him then, as I saw him as a kid in this world that was changing faster than he was able to adjust. I was smarter than he was in that regard—I was Mr. Options Open; he was pure and simple, and I was a sliding voice in hiding, keeping my crazy part from being seen at all costs—a true chameleon.

Our eyes met for a second and I felt him glance into me deeply as if he could find something, and I remember his eyes tearing up and in that moment we both knew why we had met on that day. "Well, I gotta go, Señor Cliff, *adiós* and *vaya con dios*," he added.

We shook again, I felt my grip go stronger than his for that second as if there was something reaching up from inside of me awakening. Then he left, as his stiff, awkward cowboy boots echoed off the floor.

CHAPTER 10

Meeting Norm

Friday rolled around on its own, like it usually did, and I was bone tired. Getting up at six to make it to work at six-thirty was a two-day routine for me. The morning shift meant the breakfast plates, spoons, cups, forks, and knives—scouring the porcelain free of yellow baked-on yolk that, once dried, became a chore for my green-fiber pad to separate. Somehow, the heat created a bond so protein fused to the plate like the molecules were wanting to work out their karma to the fullest, not ready to be cut short in a restaurant from that pull of life.

My thoughts ran freely above the tumbling steam of rinse water that rolled off the surface to the side of the wash basin. The logic of the dish-room filtered my left-brained thoughts and, though no sudden strokes of realization came, I was still free to make of the day what I wanted. Earning my living, going with the flow of spoons, forks, and knives in the hot soapy water, being careful not to catch the rubber gloves on the fork's prongs.

A Zen awareness enveloped me to move and be flexible to merge with the movement into a seamless flow; all this while, I was busy scouring in a zone of my own making, sometimes in the rush, when the plates were stacked up high waiting and the cups and saucers tumbled in with the rest to get clean.

The images of the stockade or a feature of one of the sergeants would come into focus and I could feel that urge to run. I'd concentrate on order and the coordination of hand and eye, and a flow would start unconsciously. Then, as the piles of plates, cups, and silverware disappeared so the beast would be broken into pieces.

I was running from the pictures, and the past was all long gone but what I feared most was being swallowed up by them. For now, I was safe here—a funny place to feel that way, so with the last plate stacked on the top shelf, I took my apron off and stretched and leaned back, reversing the strain to my back. I quietly got my timecard and punched it into the gray machine that stamped the official time that my morning shift had ended.

I walked up Cerrillos towards town past the pawn shops and motels, glancing at the glass for my reflection or peering past into the shops, wondering how someone could pawn their possessions so cheaply, probably getting thirty cents on the dollar of their value at the most—the reality that found what we as children had never ever supposed.

On to the burger-stand. I worked my way there to order a soda and play that Junior Walker song. *What does it take to win your love for me, going to play it for you*, allowing my mind to play back part of the day, editing as I went, still afraid the beast would make an appearance, in spite of my foreboding, which didn't happen, as my tired body fed not the energy required. That Indian girl didn't show, so I paid the waitress and left.

As I walked by the KFC crossing a street, the Canyon Bar came to mind. The afternoon had slid on to five o'clock and the traffic had picked up, so I walked and walked, not having any place in mind to wander to. I wasn't quite ready yet to handle the boredom of being home alone, so I kept walking til the colors of the sky started going orange and pink as the cumulus were catching the angled rays of the horizon's slide off to the west. I could see the mesas of sagebrush soft gray green countering the cotton-candy lavender of the clouds whirling by—nature's Impressionist brush that van Gogh was so good at catching. I continued by the cemetery as a little dog ran up barking, trying to get attention, which I obliged, glancing over to his owner who was trimming a hedge by one of the larger stone monuments.

The shadows were leaning, slanting much longer toward evening as I passed the School for the Deaf entrance, feeling their silence, coming to where Cerrillos and St. Michaels made an intersection with rush hour still at its peak. The cars were straining at the light, waiting for the green to signal another start on the way back home. Just prior, I saw my chance and got across before the light switched ,and I made it across in time.

Canyon Bar Return

By the time I got to the bar, it was around eight o'clock, and I was feeling tired. Sliding onto one of the barstools, I found a relaxed position. Kate was circulating between the tables, ever graceful as was her way. Mildred was behind the bar—an older complement to Kate's youth, that showed how wisdom's ability the pace oneself led to endurance, as she smiled, and wiped off the counter asking, "What'll you have?" I could feel her size me up the way one poker player would do another, silently checking for any gaps in the body language or eye contact.

I smiled, too tired to project the pretense of being something I wasn't. "Ah, I'll have a Seven and Seven, and heavy on the harder Seven," I added, figuring that right now a liquid relaxation would be good.

Her lips cracked a smile as she realized what I had meant. "That's a new one," she said, sliding the drink across the bar to me.

"I put in a full day washing dishes over at the Pantry Restaurant, and,"

"Nice to get it over with, huh?" she asked, interrupting me.

I nodded swallowing a full gulp, feeling the burning going down that spread out from my stomach and then to my brain. Someone put music on the juke box and sound erupted, *If not for you the winter would hold no spring, if not for you.* A George Harrison song unraveled its verses, and the theme struck how I did not have that someone in my life but I now had a plan. Going to the concert I'd read about on the library bulletin board would be the best way to start, as I took another drink.

I glanced around and saw the gang was beside the pool table. I didn't want to appear overanxious to be part of the group, so I stayed put and got into the music of the next tune playing, but got tired of acting cool, so I wandered over and sat down.

"Impressionism is just a hype," a tall red-haired man was saying. There was an earnestness in his voice and red stubble on his face. "It's just like," he hesitated, searching for a word to make his point. "Like hippie or groovy," he came up with, smiling at the laughter. There was a thick Norwegian accent to the way he said *groovy* that sounded ridiculous, and that was what everyone had found funny.

He glanced around, not quite realizing why they were still laughing, and a flicker of anger showed in his face, and the laughter quickly died down. You could see from his body language that this guy was wired tight. The mood of the table was much more serious than had been previously. The sarcastic tone was completely absent, as this guy was troubled.

Norm spoke up, "Jason, why are you so pissed at these categories? We all know the people who come up with labels are full of crap. It's just their job to con us into believing that they know something, when in fact, they are hustling and they just aren't going to stop. That's the way it is, and we just have get used to it." He said seriously.

"Some jerk at the gallery said my work was Neo-Impressionist, and there was no demand for that old style of painting anymore."

"And that's what pissed you off," Norm asked, pinning him down.

Jason nodded, "The piece was a Still Life, for heaven sakes, not Neo." The pitch of his voice rose so that you could see there was a hurt.

"So, the guy was too busy typing for him to see the beauty it held, is that it?" Norm asked, taking a deep breath and waiting. Norm was going on a hunch; the table fell silent and waited.

Jason took a long drink from his glass and nodded his head, took a sigh and looked into his glass of beer bubbles rising.

"Easy, Jason, not everyone likes my poetry, and they categorize it, but I don't let that get to me. Heck, if I let it get me, I'd go crazy. Anyhow, with poetry you get rejections and 'good luck next time'."

"You ask me," Clyde chimed in, "the whole capitalism system sucks. All they're interested in is whether or not they can make a buck."

Norm nodded, adding, "Good one, Clyde—the power of the dollar. Everyone has got their bottom line that they worry about. But, you know that we love what we do, and people like it enough so they'll spend money, and that puts us out of their reach. In a way, what pisses them off the most is that we're independent. They can't touch us."

Clyde interjected, "They say Cezanne tore up hundreds of his work, just because of one flaw that no one else saw was not quite right. To us it's about matching vision with the reality is just what we do"

"Either it's the words or the pigments, and it comes from here." Norm raised his fist to his chest and hit it to emphasize his point. The accented movement stood out in an extraordinary manner.

Jason glanced, nodding his head while he acknowledged the truth, which struck a chord in all of us, since we were all nodding intently. I was having a hard time with the ebbs and flows of the dialogue.

Norm's eyes lit up a bit, showing that ideas were formulating, "They say that a normal person has to face his death once a month, but a creative person has to face it at least every five days or so."

I was making a connection about creativity and Buddhism's nirvana but my thoughts were just too scattered to come up with a concept. It was close enough for me, as my heart kicked in a gear *kerthump, kerthump* that I thought everyone could hear, as I got ready. "Dylan Thomas wrote that poem about death not having dominion." My words popped out before I could even continue with a tie-in.

The table turned to me accepting what I had said so far and waited a split second for me to draw a transition for it to fit. "It's a paradox thing," I was hanging by a thread. "That very thing that fires us to go further out, in the end has no real power over us, I'm trying to say," I struggled and felt good at the same time. I took a deep breath, waited, and felt my heart kicking into high gear.

"Yes," Norm said. "It does and then it doesn't, like a true paradox. It's like salt, too much hides the flavors, too little the food is bland. What we're after is that balance," he added, kissing his fingertips, adding, "the way French cooks do when they achieve that *coup de grace.*"

Clyde stroked his mustache, the whole time looking in the distance. "They say," he broke the silence, "that the high the heroin gives you is just the result of the metabolic chaos the drug causes your body and that the rush you feel is adrenalin kicking in to reestablish order. The reality gap one feels when all this is going on allows that high."

"True," Norm interjected, "after the first time, it's never the same, chasing that dragon, is what a junkie is after for the rest of his life."

"Here's to first times," Jason said, holding his drink high for a toast. Which we pretty much did in unison and we took a long drink.

"If it wasn't for those first times," Norm said, "I'd look a lot younger." The table went quiet and I leaned shifting my weight in my chair. "Where you from?" Norm asked, looking in my direction, hesitating.

I could feel the moment had arrived for me to introduce myself, "Paonia, Colorado," I said, "Dad retired from the Navy, got a ranch but he sold it and moved to Florida, so now I'm not from anywhere, you could say. I'm here because I love it. I also write poems and I get a kick out of listening to you guys and stretching my ideas."

"You ever get published?" he asked with an intent look on his face.

"Yes, I got a couple published in a penny poetry down in Boulder."

Norm took a swig from his beer and swallowed, then taking a breath, "I'm going to start a poetry reading at the Mt. Ararat coffee house off Alameda, on the lower west side of San Francisco Street." He added, "It will start, yes, this Thursday. You ought to come by and read what you got." He finished and took another sip of his beer and then leaned back. "I used to live in Frisco but city life got to me, so I left, but I did have some good times."

I could see in the back of his eyes while he talked that it was true, in the part that he still carried with him, reading poetry late nights in smoky café's with Ferlinghetti slinging words like gunfighters. He held his hand out, we shook and looked into each other's eyes, one poet to another mingling fingers and words in a no name bar. "I'm Norm Moser, glad to meet you," he said.

"My name is Cliff Alexander and glad to meet you too," I said smiling, and just like that, a key link was in place and I didn't even realize it. I had enough for this night and felt the tiredness of the day come through my body, thinking now about the long walk home. "Thank you," I said, scanning the group, as I politely walked out.

CHAPTER 11

The Concert

Sunday and seven-thirty rolled around with my mind full of both expectation and determination, as I walked into the dark room and found a spot. As my eyes adjusted, I could make out dark forms here and there where people were sitting, and I got right to work checking silhouettes for any single unattached ladies while the band played a song.

I found a likely prospect, and quietly moved beside to where she was. "Pretty good sounds," I said to her, speaking loud enough to get heard.

"Not bad," she said, looking back at me in a nonchalant cool way. That didn't get it, since I was looking for good vibes. I wasn't going to waste my time like I did in college days hanging out with the gang at Tulagi's on The Hill at Boulder where I learned how to get humbled by a table full of pretty girls.

No way, I thought, going to the left side of the audience, squinting hard as I could into the dimly lit room, still determined to find her. I zeroed in on one with long dark hair who was keeping time, bobbing her head into the rhythm, obviously having a good time. I leaned over toward her and said, "Pretty good drummer, huh?"

She glanced over her shoulder in my direction to check me out. Leaning toward me, she put her finger to her lips, saying nothing. Her body language spoke to me with one of those girl- paradox things, where her lips were saying *no, no* while her body was saying *yes, yes*, which was all I needed, so I held position and got quietly animated.

She glanced back later in my direction to verify her first impression. I must have passed, since she could have moved somewhere else but stayed and held to that decision that I had forced on her. I saw her relax and start clicking her fingers, getting into the beat, which I too found myself getting into the rhythm, nodding my head.

The band, however, was really terrible, as they had little connection, which meant the drummer and the lead guitar were out of sync, and the singer compensated by singing louder above the mistakes. They played with intensity that made them look pretty comical. Things were good, so I figured that it was no big deal. I was happy right up to their final song and that awkward moment when I looked at her and said, "Hello, my name's Cliff Alexander."

She smiled and glanced in a noncommittal sort in my direction. "Mine's Jan," just loud enough for me to make out.

"Would you like to get a drink over at the La Fonda," I asked.

She hesitated, thought, and said, "Why not, I like that place."

It was a cold as we went outside and felt the wind on our faces walking down the Governor's Palace front sidewalk, going east where we crossed a street and went by trading posts with their wares displayed in the windows and by a gallery and a clothing store. She walked with a detached stride, hands in her pockets.

"You go to school?" I asked as we slowed, looking at her expression.

"Yes," she said, admiring a dress in a store display that made the manikin look shapely. As she stood there, I saw from her side that she had an ample shape herself.

"What?" Jan said, seeing me looking at her in the window's reflection.

"Oh, I was thinking that that dress would look good on you," I said, as we turned around and started walking.

"Have you been in Santa Fe long?" she asked as we crossed a street.

"I got here in August and stayed at this commune until it closed down."

"What do you do?" she asked, as we entered the La Fonda's door. A clock over the check-in counter read nine. "Ah *crap*," she stopped mid track, "I didn't know it was this late. Would you mind walking me home instead? I've got an eight o'clock tomorrow and I'm not good at getting up. The school's across town."

I backed up and followed her quicker step. "That's one thing I've got a lot of, and I, no, I'd like to walk you home."

"What's that?" she said, as we made our way across the park. "That you've got plenty of?" she queried, taking a good look at me.

I took my time as if I was pondering her question, letting her study my features, feeling confident that my symmetry would hold up to her scrutiny, as we walked on San Francisco past the old theater. "Time," I said with enthusiasm, "I've got plenty of time."

We walked over sidewalks past houses of the west-side barrio, and I listened, how her dad had married a black women in Watts, and how she had to grow up fast in that black community's values, always taking heat from the chicks, and being hustled by the guys. Through it all, she didn't get much rest but she had managed.

As I glanced while she went on, I saw a certain set to her jaw that showed a sense of power as she described her situation and found a confidence to her step and stride as she went on with her descriptions. I was viewing how raw courage plays out in body language. Funny, how much you learn about a person walking them home.

We came to where Alameda hits St. Francis and walked across to the corner where we walked up to a house and she unlocked the door. "Well, this is my home," she said, opening the lock and looking back. "Would you like to go out with me?" I asked in a nonchalant way.

She stepped in her doorway then turned. "Okay," she answered.

"Great, I'll be by for you around eight o'clock," I said, turning to go.

"Excuse me," she said, breaking my step so that I had to stop short, adding, "mind telling me which day it will be. Be nice to know."

"Oh, Friday. I'll be by for you Friday," I repeated, shaking my head.

The next day my speed was back with the silverware and plates. Thinking without thinking—Zen in the dish room, allowing my hands to go with the feel, as the souring pad worked, and I went back to my meeting with Jan and how easy it had been. Even Trudy, the grouchy waitress, said the plates were immaculate and that there had been no backup, like times before.

The radio was playing loudly on its perch on top of the water pipes with the duct tape securing just where the pipes went into the wall. "*One bad apple don't spoil the whole bunch, boy, da, da,*" came out

As I reached for the next dirty dish to the rhythm of the song and slid it in the suds, as it went under and bumped on the bottom, I thought of her figure. I allowed fantasies to work in my mind, then got pulled to reality when hot water ran over my glove. I couldn't help but wonder at how well things were falling into place.

The fear hadn't left since, like the plates that were under the suds, that beast was there, as I still felt a foreboding, split-seconds away. I still had to keep the motion going since it was the only thing that kept it at bay.

Poetry at the Mt. Ararat Coffee House

Sure enough, it was right as Norm had said—near the Laundromat. I sat at a table that was once a telephone cable spool. The talk was that Jeanne, a singer of a local band called Cramps, had a rich father who was giving her this platform where she could perfect her singing and become a success. It worked out for us that since Thursdays were free, Norm had plugged in the idea of making it a free poetry night, and the rest is history.

Norm walked on the stage and adjusted the mike, saying, "Good evening," to the audience. "Also fellow poets," he added, making a special effort to scan faces. Seeing me, he nodded and turning, did the same to someone else. "Welcome to poetry night at Mt. Ararat Coffee House. I'd like to start this session with one I call *Prancing Around*."

> Bumping burgers between buns pickles and onions
> Flip flop French fries tongues flicking with catsup
> Swig a coke wash it down flavors meshed up alive
> Watching the waitress work her magic of curves
> Smiles come-ons just enough to sense there's more
> Up and down the aisles in her realm of orders and tips

The special of the day "I just know you'd like it,"
She'd say, popping her juicy fruit gum jotting down
Shorthand of what's your pleasure on a platter
Knowing all the time who's ready to pay the tab
Or who's ready to order or wants some dessert
Bouncing or the mesh of nylon all at once moving
She keeps it fresh coming at you, staccato Nancy
Queen of the Curly Q Diner in her hiking boots.

Norm held his gaze out into the audience and said, "Thank you." I wasn't used to his free association of words that spun fast like there's no stopping them with their fury of style over tradition. You might say I was dumbfounded, as having had a sheltered life, coming in contact only with Wordsworth or Poe or Frost in high school classes. I had no idea that any other kind of poetry existed.

This was poetry for the sake of poetry, words for their sound first and their meaning a close second, or dangling no meaning at all. I watched, quietly transfixed you might say at his confidence, like he was saying, *Come and get me, if you can, I'm right here.* So I watched for how he delivered his lines, sometimes smiling. Sometimes, he'd hold back a word like he didn't want to let it go, and the hesitation at the time had no relationship to the rest passing through the next line. Almost like it was an afterthought, only to see, that the poem had needed a pause or slower speed. He was full of paradoxes, never predicable, and that was his power. He held you by the sheer strength of his character and zest of life. Then just like that, it was over, with him just standing there with his thick mustache and wide forehead hunched over the mike, leaning on the mike's stand like a huge bear protecting his territory, not giving one inch as if driven into the stage, and then bowed and took a seat.

The café tables glittered with fluttering candle flames that sent silhouettes of patrons to the walls, their three dimensions falling darkly, each with distinct rhythm as my heart kicked up a notch. I knew what that was telling me, so I took a breath, stood and unfolded my shaky stack of papers and went up, my hand holding the paper shaking badly.

"Hello, I'm Cliff Alexander, and I've got a couple of poems for you." Here goes, past the point of no return, taking a deep breath.

The sky ran through the trees vibrating leaves
Raising and lowering limbs fluttering like birds
A thousand wings held to the tethered branches
Walking under them with my collar turned up
I remember what you said that morning ago
Last night about us tangled in the dark shadows
Half whispered like this wind now around me
I will wait for you, I could just make them out
Any lower and I wouldn't have known at all
And I can feel now their pull with the winds
What was it in the syllables of your breath
Why now I can't let them go, why I hold on
Like those leaves beating in their places
All you are of those words lipless in my mind
But I will find you and trace them back up
What I lost of me that's not but once was
That morning so very long and distant ago.

I stopped and waited, looking out as Norm had done quietly. There was a force in the clapping that told me I'd struck a chord. "Thank you," I said, and found my place among the spools. I felt my heart settle down to a normal pattern.

Then this guy with ruffled hair and a dark shirt with dark features walked over, rubbing his hands on the sides of his shirt. He had horn-rimmed glasses perched right on the end of his nose, which he brushed back up on his nose as he got near he mike. He looked down on the stack of papers he had set on the podium. One at a time, he looked over them like he was meeting a friend, then he turned to the mike and said, "I got a couple I want to share." He went up with an independent attitude that made him stand out. He had this absoluteness that I admired, an indifference that told everyone he had his own reasons for being up there. He projected with a voice that rang with clarity and distinctness.

You are so much like the coffee you know
With your skin of mahogany full of richness
Swallowing me up in one glance like a thirst
So when you speak I lean on your expression
Wired long past the caffeine nerves this touch
Shaky in my throat what I'm afraid most of
So that you'll never know how my heart beats
In between your silent way of holding me fast
That next sentence words full of just enough
The power you have of oblivion's so close next
In my voice so you'll think it isn't there at all
But I know you know as I stand in front of you
This all that is everything and leaves not out
Even this boy whose face I've long forgotten
Was once even him you own in your hand
And climbs when I'm alone so I can't stand it
Why I hold you so close why I can't let go
When the night shines off your breath words
These empty cups now on the kitchen counter
Stained with your lipstick a pale red glow
The part about gone that flavors the moment
The obvious that is written on my face
And between the lines echoes in my heart
That subside between your heartbeats now
So that all I can think is that I want more of you

81

And how that won't be enough but it'll do.

He stopped and you could almost sense us holding our breath with the way he had spoken each word, bringing out its secrets, where sound and inflection mixed meaning and breathed life into the words. Such was his way and as unkempt as he was, it didn't matter. He nodded acknowledgement of the applause in an embarrassed way, and he bowed meekly and sat down.

Golly, that guy was too much, good beyond good. I felt envious and small at the same time after hearing him. I was pretty good but he had real talent.

Norm got on the raised platform, grabbed the mike and said, "I know it's late, so let me introduce our poets for this night. We have over there pointing to me, Cliff Alexander from Paonia." Pointing across the room, "There's David Goldstein. My name is Norm Moser, and we'll be doing this every Thursday, so put that on your calendars and bring poems if you got'um."

Then, just like that, people disappeared into the night. I glanced over at David and he gave me a nod and I nodded back, but I was just too afraid to go over to formally introduce myself. So, my long walk back to my garage apartment silently began past the barking dogs and the shaking pods of locust trees with the moon hanging silver in the crystal black sparkling sky. This lone guy with his own crystal glowing silver made of words discovered how words had triggered this flame that gave him joy and something new, something he hadn't experienced before was happening.

The night took on this sudden spark that, though it was ageless, at the same time it had become all so new and thrillingly alive.

CHAPTER 13

Friday's Date

I walked over, smelling of Aqua Velva, Dial soap, and Ban deodorant, so that I had all my bases well covered—(first impressions you know). Anyhow, Jan invited me in as she finished up putting her makeup on like she was letting me see her in action, making final preparations. She ran a comb through her hair, smiling as the strands crackled with static electricity. I smiled at her and took in her figure in a black dress. She added a red scarf around her neck that gave a hint of fashion. I noticed her curves contoured the black fabric into hills and valleys.

With one last look in the mirror she smiled and declared, "All ready." She gave me her arm and out the door we went, ready for the night, walking toward her gray Valiant. She gave me the keys as we got near, and I opened the door for her, got in and inserted the keys turning them.

"You know how to drive with a stick," Jan leaned over toward me, asking.

I got a whiff of this perfume I hadn't smelled before, and I was in trouble, as my mind had disjointed from her question, and came up blank. "Ah yes," I said, turning the key, shifting into reverse, letting out the clutch. Then heading to the street, I shifted into second gear, grinding as I did.

"Second gear will do that, but it's okay, happens all the time," she added.

I knew the town pretty much from the walking I'd done in three months, so I figured out a route and navigated the narrow streets pretty well. I could feel the tension of her body near mine as I made different turns, and either I'd be leaning on her and her on me, which felt pretty good. When we got to Canyon Bar, the band had already was all set up, and was ready to go. We found a table and ordered drinks and smiled at each other, pretty much not sure what to expect next as the band got into a song.

Hey Mister Tambourine Man, play a song for me, I'm not sleepy, and. The singer sang with the same intensity of the drummer, lead guitar, and before long, Jan and I were both moving to the music.

"Want'a dance?" I asked across the table, already knowing the answer.

She nodded and I took her hand, and we waded into the rolling sound as if we were facing the breakers on a beach pounding toward us. As Jan danced with confidence, I was pulled likewise. It didn't matter if it was a tsunami, we were locked and loaded body surfing, mingling with the drummer's play off the rhythm guitar, so we were able to improvise in and out of the flowing sound. Whatever forever is made of, that's what we were slipping into. I'd get closer and suddenly she would turn away and look back, holding her look just enough to show me she wasn't going to be easy. At the same time, it told me I had something that caused this spin- generating electricity so our magnetos were meshing each other's present-tense magic, that this was happening to us. When the band stopped for a break, we left the floor arm in arm.

We ambled back to our table and drank deeply, sensing our thirst, feeling the burn of the alcohol find its place in my stomach spread. Then as I caught my breath, I felt a slowing down of my thinking, a pondering shift of my conscious, and I glanced at Jan and smiled.

"What?" she asked, leaning forward to hear what my response was.

"You're a pretty good dancer," I said, nodding my head approvingly.

"You haven't seen nothing yet. I'm just warming up," she added.

"Where'd you learn your moves? You're pretty good too," she said.

"Over at Tulagi's in Boulder. FAC on Fridays I'd dance all afternoon. I've always loved to dance to good music, can't help it." As I was talking, in the background the band started.

I looked at her and motioned about going out, and she nodded yes, and we got out there. With the benefit of the Seagram's flux, I lingered more into a rhythm than before. It became something like automatic-transmission music translating into motion where the time became like butter melting as we flowed into the rhythms when they're blending and coming apart all at once so that we lost track.

Different dynamics made a dialogue work all the aspects, so that our eyes read a language before the words could come out. Poetry of motion spontaneously came as the music wound a web. I could tell from the amount of pressure her hand allowed for me to hold, or the resistance suo that I felt the pull of her thoughts, how she played me impartially enough to allow me to wonder then how her detached look went, until her long hair brushed my hand soft as a whisper so that I had thought she had said something. As I leaned closer to hear, she noticed and laughed.

Moths to the Light Bulb

85

As a slow song came up, we felt our bodies sway and step and adjust to rhythm and motion midst the electricity. Drawing closer like moths to a light bulb, we went fearlessly pulled. That hint of her perfume, which I imagined falling endlessly into came softly, as did the feel of her body against mine all round me. She held me steady with a slight pressure, enough to pull me closer.

The magic was winding in the music magnets finding north poles, mercury flowing liquid, rolling warmth and spreading all over with the give, in how she followed and resisted, both at the same time. Our two bodies were orbiting the music, operating to our own gravity, and so it continued with the give and take, discovering as we went what could have gone on forever, weightless time thus suspended.

"Break time," the singer said, as they finished the song.

We went to the table and sipped our drinks and I stretched out. She had given some secret away out there on the dance floor and was disguising it now with an indifferent look as she drank, then getting up, she said, "Going to the ladies room. I'll be back."

I watched has Jan slipped between the tables, chairs, and people. Something in her movements reminded me of velvet, akin to the way a spider weaves her web out of a thread that comes from this sac in her belly, spinning strands of silken silver that brought this weightless feeling in my mind. As she came back, she looked better than before, as now there was this certain air of confidence that made her hold a steady glance into my eyes that I had to break. She sat down and crossed her legs with the sound of nylon on nylon.

"So how was it living in Watts?" I asked, noticing how her eyes sparkled "Oh, I had to learn lot of lessons in a short amount of time," she added, "like where not to hang out, or who to stay away from, and what's okay, what's not, and how to pick up the real vibes of a situation that would decide all the rest. Yes, you could say it was a challenging time for me." she asked, "How about you growing up in a small town in Colorado?"

"Ah, I was pretty lucky since I had all this freedom around me. Everything made sense in its season, and I enjoyed the hard work." I said, looking back on those hard days with a certain pride. "In fact, if Dad hadn't sold the place, I'd be there right now working."

"You're a long way from that farm right now. Huh," she said smiling.

"Yes, maybe I've grown, and it would've been time to leave anyhow," I said, thinking about how right now, my freedom seemed paramount. "Think you'll go back to Watts, after you get your degree?" I asked.

"That's a good question. I don't know except I like this place a lot."

The band came back and started playing rock with an easier beat. We worked our way to an open spot on the dance floor. There was a relaxed way about how we fell into the beat without trying, like something was behind us from which we could proceed forward.

We danced enough and sat down again, this time sitting near each other. Later I got this warm phosphorescent feeling, and I put my arm around Jan and could feel her strong solid presence alive, and I thought about this little girl thrown there in the middle of Watts. "Want to leave?" I asked, whispering in her ear, smelling that perfume.

She nodded yes, and we made our way through the maze of tables outside where our breaths went grey as we went to the car. I navigated through the narrow streets and parked beside her house, turned the engine off, and leaned over and kissed her soft and smooth.

She nodded yes, when I pulled away and asked if I could come. We slid the key in the lock and opened it. I walked in behind her while she took off her coat and went to stereo. While I sat down on the sofa, she put on a Stones album. *You can't always get what you want, but if you try sometimes…* played on. We danced to the music and came closer and closer til our lips touched, and in sequences that followed, we found how darkness can be like light and that sleep was an ocean we swam in, out past where the breakers appeared where we dove deep drowning in each other's thirst until it quenched and our dreams found us sailing places that spun from way before we met.

The next morning I told her I had to get out and walk up to the square.

"I'm having a test on Monday, so I'm going to study over the weekend. What if I see you about the same time next Friday?" she said, kissing me. I leaned against her and felt the mercury of the moment move, then go. I looked at her and she smiled and looked over at her books on the table.

I went to the square and found Penguin's studio on San Francisco west of Walgreens on the opposite side of the street up the stairs. Penguin had *The Boxer* song by Simon and Garfunkel on the stereo and the volume turned up so he didn't notice me coming in. I saw him bent over a canvas working with his brush and oil paints. The smell of turpentine came as I got closer and saw the picture he was working on was a bear swiping at a salmon. There was a lot of motion to the painting—flowing rapids, splashes, the paw of the bear still submersed in the water and the fish there.

Penguin saw me and looked up from the middle of a brush stroke to smile. He then turned to the work and worked with the water. I turned and saw Buffy working on a pine branch with a hacksaw, intent on working with the grains to flesh out a figure. He nodded to let me know he knew that I was here, as I pulled out my steno notebook from the Rainbow Bread bag and found a place at the end of a table and let the words come as the song worked its chorus over and over building up intensity. Words flowed off my pen about Sue the Cook.

Sue the Cook

Sue the chef of the commune mix of humanity
Somewhere in the blend of the spices and sauce
She was there where on the tip of your tongue
The flavors came together just so with uniqueness
And you wondered what were her special secrets
And as you tried to find them out you also saw
What great care she put to cover them with chaos
That day in day out you came to look forward
Her grand delights could make a simple stew
Fit for a king this melding of skill and creativity
Carrots, onions, a slice of cheese and that spice
That you came to expect the best that could
Of what little she came up with would be
Sue the goodwill cook that gave her all for joy
She saw in us as we partook of her savory dishes
Sue with the touch that made food come alive
Whose touch that night I helped little Andrea
Me to see there was something I too had
Our meeting whose meanings hold as long
As these words can reach their fire there free
Slender and transfixed with a same longed love.

I finished the poem, as *The Boxer* song played over and over, and suddenly I was overcome and got emotional. Buffy came over curious about what was making me sad. I looked away and thought to that night in the kitchen.

"She was lucky you were there," I remember her saying, and I smiled at Buffy and put my steno notebook in the wonder bag I always had tucked under my belt. I glanced up at the clock on the wall by the south-facing window. It read seven-thirty, and I was surprised how the time had passed by.

"Hey, what'a you say we get something to eat?" I yelled over to Buffy who looked up from his carving and glanced at Penguin who smiled.

"Who's buying?" Penguin said pulling himself away from his painting.

"I got paid this week so I've got some money," I chimed in, feeling big.

"Let's go then," Buffy said with his usual sense of finality and drama.

Didn't take us long to get to the Taco Bell just down from the old pad.

"You heard about the party?" Penguin said, biting into his tostada.

"Yeah, Veronica and her sister aren't there anymore," Buffy added.

"I never did like Veronica much," I said eating my taco supreme, "So then, what are we waiting for?" I added glancing at the cashier who was a pretty Spanish girl with a slender body and ready smile.

"Maybe after we get done, we could go over see if it got started?" Buffy said, adding, "Let's pick up Budweiser at that store."

So, I spent seven dollars getting two six packs and we headed to the pad that had made all the difference way back when I had needed it. Way back on that lonely rainy night when it was my time.

The party was underway. Going up the driveway, we could hear *Rolling on the River* by Credence. When we walked in, people glanced at us but paid no mind at all as some were dancing, laughing, conversing or making out. I grabbed chips and a can of that Budweiser we had bought and noticed a petite Spanish-looking girl with long straight dark hair, high cheek bones, pouty lips, flashing dark eyes, and nice curves, standing all by herself over beside the stereo that blared the music.

I wandered over within ear shot, "You like Credence?" I asked her.

"Well, for the first hundred times, yes, but," she smiled, hesitated.

"The second hundred, the song has lost some zip, huh?" I added.

"Yes, you could say that," she said, taking a sip of her can of Coors, "I think I've got it pretty much memorized now."

I put a strained look on my face and moved to the beat, mocking it.

She laughed, showing beautiful white teeth and a clear complexion. As she leaned back, she emphasizing the bulges beneath her blouse. Her body language spoke of youth in itsdefiant stance. Her brown eyes had a Castilian bend to her brows and a gypsy flare, all blended at once as she glanced around at the group around us.

"What music do you like?" I asked her, feeling a sense of acceptance.

"Anything that has a beat. I love to dance when I'm in the mood."

"What about now?" I said, picking up the beat of the song.

"Nah, not now, I don't like to stand out and be the only one," she said.

"Are you here looking for anybody special?" I said, looking around.

91

"Nah, I just heard that there was a party, decided to check it out.

How about you?" she countered, scanning my face.

"I know Buffy from when I used to crash here about a month ago," I said,

"He told me about the party and I figured, what the heck, go over."

"Pretty odd, you being an Anglo and all," she said a matter-of-factly.

I laughed. "I don't consider myself an Anglo." I said, glancing at Buffy.

"How do you figure that?" she said, seeing my connection with Buffy.

I hesitated, trying to come up with something, "I'm not sure." I said.

She didn't say anything for a while, got into the beat, and laughed,

"That could be the reason, most Anglos always. . . ," she started to say.

"Always what?" I interrupted, being a little defensive with her flow.

"Always have a ready answer for what they do, and want to tell it." She said smiling into my eyes, "You're different, I'll admit to that." Adding, "I don't usually," she began speaking again, sipping her beer.

"Don't usually what?" I interrupted, sensing my mistake immediately.

"Don't allow myself to, well, to talk to any Anglo who comes along." She said giving me a perturbed look for interrupting her like I'd done.

I withdrew my energy, and just studied her eyes and her full pink lips. "I'm Cliff Alexander," I said, holding out my hand ready to take hers.

Which she offered gracefully, saying, "My name is Consuela Rosales."

There was a suppleness to the way she allowed me to hold her hand, a certain confidence in who she was that came through.

"Would you like to go for a walk and get out of here," I asked.

"Sounds pretty good," she said, looking around, getting her coat.

I put mine on and helped her with hers, and gave Buffy a wave. He nodded at me and glanced at Consuela and looked away. We exited and felt the cold as it turned our breaths powdery blue that billowed up above us into the air as we walked on the drive under the light post where we took a right and headed toward the square. Above, the night air was full of the smell of fireplaces burning red that sent the smell of pine, cedar, or pinon fragrances to our noses. The sky sparkled with the gaps and stars bent out in the Milky Way. In the cold air we walked closer together to share our body heat.

As we got to the square, it was easy to see no one else felt our same urgeto get out and feel the way the elements mixed with the frigid air. The benches stood vacant under the streetlights—a somber sign that a storm might be ready to cut loose.

We soon got cold and shivered and headed to the La Fonda. We walked into the lobby and took a right went down a long hallway that ran along a closed-off patio that was vacant with empty tables, and at the end of the hall we took a left and went into a large room that in the center of its wall had a large fireplace with a fire burning.

We sat facing the orange flames that were licking the sides of a log going up full yellow orange cracking with sparks, which would shoot out onto the tile in front of us and burn out sending a trail of grey smoke. We felt the infrared on our hands as we held them outstretched. Her face had a ruddy color to it and noticing my stare, she smiled, and I found myself being drawn to her the same way I was to the fire. Seeing how the light highlighted the angled contours of her face and the fleshed parts of her neck and face a deep tanned brown. I drew a blank in the middle of my unconscious study of her face.

"You warm?" she asked, interrupting my scanning of her scenery.

"I'm getting that way," I responded, pulling my gaze to the fire.

She leaned toward the fire like a cat does arching its back.

We wandered over to a painting hanging on the wall that had a group of Indians gathered by an adobe house in winter since there was a trail of grey smoke coming out of the chimney, and in the background there was a silhouette of a dark mountain and above it a night sky that was full of stars and a half moon. The magic of the artist's skill held us both in awe.

"I wonder what the Indians are thinking right then?" she asked.

"Let me see," I said, "Probably, how cold that it is out there."

"I'm not so sure from the way that they are standing there," she said in a thoughtful way.

"They could be seeing the beauty."

I was struck by the fresh way that she interpreted the picture. There was no hint of lack of certainty in the way she spoke or any haughtiness from the fact that she could be right on.

We walked on to the next work of art that was a portrait of a matriarch near a fireplace in a dark dress. It was done in somber tones, that gave it a feeling of repose.

"There's sadness. See her eyes, and how she's holding her hands as if she is trying to hide something from those she loves. Let's move on, this one is getting to me," Consuela said, adding, "It reminds me too much of my grandmother except for the looks."

"Yes, that artist was good to bring that out like he did," I added.

We continued our tour of the art that was hanging in the hallways, walking easily among the guests as if we were paying customers. A bellboy came by that I recognized from somewhere. He stopped abruptly and walked up to me smiling, "*Ola*," he said smiling and holding out his hand for me to shake, which I did. "*Recuerda usted, recuerda de la hospital in la emergencia?*" he said.

"Oh," I said and just then it hit me that this was the guy I helped that first week I was at the ER, who came in with a busted-up leg. Then smiling, I gave him a warm handshake and smiled back.

He hugged me and kept saying, "*Muchas gracias, muchas gracias.*"

"*De nada*," I remembered from my Spanish class to say in return.

He then went about what he was doing prior to bumping in us. And finding ourselves warm, we walked on, heading for the exit.

"Who was that?" Consuela asked, looking back as the guy disappeared.

"Someone I helped out when I was working at the emergency room. He came in with a busted-up leg that had got infected in a bad way. A doctor was just going to give him a shot and send him on his way, but I worked it out so that another doctor looked at the wound

,and that way he was able to get officially admitted to the hospital. So, you might say, he remembers that pretty good, huh?" I asked.

"That was nice of you. So you're good with Chicanos too?" she asked

"Ah, that's how I was raised. You help anyone who needs it," I said.

She gave me a deeper look as if she was trying to read if that was real and she nodded and we proceeded out of the doorway. The night was like it had been before—crystal clear with stars twinkling. Our breaths mixed up grey blue clouds that dissipated into nothing as we headed down San Francisco and checked out the shops, giving theories as to whether a man or woman had put it together. Nothing escaped our eye down to the smallest detail of the setup.

"See the way the female mannequin's eyes don't meet," she went on. "Shows that a guy put it together, plus that he hated his mother."

We both laughed that it really sounded plausible out of the blue as if we were great critics, as well as a psychological specialists. We both got more and more bizarre with our comments, laughing, having a good time, we had long lost any track of time or location.

Uuuh ooooh. Suddenly just like that, there was a flashlight in our faces blinding us.

"What are you two doing out way past the curfew?" he demanded. It was a police officer who stood there with the flashlight in our eyes, making it certain that he wasn't going to let up on the pressure.

"Here, let me see," he added, looking close right at Consuelo's face, "Why, Consuelo Rosales. Does your dad know you're out this late?" He added then turning the flashlight on my face in a serious manner.

Oh *crap*, this can't be happening to me. I was in shock.

"Let me see some ID," he said in an accusatory tone like I was a criminal. "Do you know, this is called contributing to the delinquency of a minor? Mister Alexander. In fact, you are way past the curfew hour." He added. "Not good," he added, as if he was ready to lock me up right away.

My mouth was way past being dry, desiccated would be a better word. The switch from the lackadaisical mood I had been on to this was a shock, and the cop was showing no signs from not making this to be a big deal. The flashbacks of the stockade began barraging my fragile state of mind. All that I had left behind was right there in that light in my face.

"I just came from a party," I stammered hoping to change the subject.

"You remember where?" he asked, letting up that tough tone in his voice.

I nodded my head yes, and he motioned me to follow him to his squad car.

I directed him through the streets right to the driveway in front, and we could hear the party was still going good as we got closer. We got to the door, whereupon he rapped loudly with his hand *ala* a cop. As the door cracked open, the officer went in and the party went silent.

"I'm afraid this party has been disturbing the peace," he roughly stated, "And I need to see some ID's," he added looking around at everybody.

Luckily, everyone had an ID that he checked. He took his time with each one, to let everyone know he was in control, after which he added gruffly, "Well, you got to keep the noise down. Next time I come out, I'll be locking someone for a stay in the slammer."

We followed him out, avoiding all mean stares that were coming our way. We got in the squad car and he turned the lights off and drove us to near Consuelo's house.

"And you two, you better get Consuelo home pronto, right?" he added. He took off leaving us standing alone on the gravel drive with me aware of my mortality. Turns out that Consuelo lived just up from where I did near the school. After I left her at her door, I walked home with the phantoms aroused. Needless to say, I had a long sleepless night, saved by the breaking dawn.

Another time I was saved by the spoons, knives, and spoons along with the plates and the cups, which all brought me around to a semblance of order from the spin I was in. The cop's face and the certainty in his voice about locking me up stayed, but here I was in the middle of the morning rush, holding on strong. You might say I had dodged a bullet, the bullet would have finished me I could see, as I thought about how close I had come that I had to focus and keep pushing past the shaking that wanted to spread up my hand.

I never was so happy for the heavy morning rush or Linda's stern face. I could feel a scratchiness coming to my throat, along with a deep cough. That unexpected exposure to cold deep night air had taken its toll, and I could tell the beginning signs and that tomorrow I was going to have to stay inside to head off the cold.

CHAPTER 14

Getting Sick

My neighbor Elizabeth poked her head in my room, hesitating while I coughed. "You don't sound good. You're staying with us tonight," she said with a tone in her voice that told me her mind had been made up, adding, "What you need is my good chicken soup, that'll fix you up." She nodded her head and walked off with her hair in that bun. That's the way she was, she didn't know how to ask, she just knew.

She let me have her room in the middle of the larger house. The one door came right off the larger room near the bathroom. The other rooms came from a hallway that dead-end in the bathroom. I was nervous about being the only guy around a bunch of crazy ladies, and all sorts of weird ideas ran in my mind, especially in my condition. Since the lock on the door didn't work, I got hangers out of the closet and hung them on the doorknob and moved the dresser so that when the door opened, the hangers rattle.

Then, with my early-warning system activated, I relaxed and went to sleep. Around three o'clock in the morning, someone's walking woke me up. The squeaking of the floorboard preceded the weak turning of the knob and the just audible sound of the hinges moving till the hangers hit the dresser, which noise surprised the intruder so that the door stopped creaking, and it got quietly pushed shut. Then the house fell silent again.

In the morning, I had to admit it that the warmth of the house had worked. The warm air and sound sleep had been what I had needed—I felt better. I heard a knock and the door opened as I had removed the hangers earlier.

Elizabeth came in with a bowl of soup with a spinning cloud of steam that rolled up and out as she came in and set it on the nightstand. "Be careful," she said, "it's still hot and it'll burn your tongue."

As I ate, sure to take little spoonful's, Elena came in and sat on the bed.

"How'd the moron catch a cold?" she asked, running her fingers in her hair.

"Just a second," I said, thinking about her riddle and taking sip of soup. My mind wasn't working so sharp, so I shrugged saying, "I don't know."

"He didn't catch it stupid, it caught him." She said with a triumphant tone.

Elena stood up and walked to the mirror on the nightstand and admired herself up and down with a careful eye.

"Do you think I'm too big?" she asked, adding, "Elizabeth says I'm too big."

I coughed more and swallowed another spoonful of soup.

Elizabeth looked in the door. "Elena, can't you tell he's sick?" she said in a loud voice that interrupted Elena's moment of admiration, adding, "He's not going to get better with you bothering him like a mother hen. Go finish your housework, that you haven't done."

"You ain't gonna boss me!" Elena said to Elizabeth as she turned to leave.

"How'd you like the soup?" Elizabeth said, getting the bowl.

"You know, you cook real good, Elizabeth," I said, pulling the covers up.

A smile came to her lips that she hid as she pulled the door shut. I lay there a while looking at the ceiling, going in and out of sleep. I woke up to a loud conversation between Elizabeth and a Spanish lady. The conversation was highlighted with the clicking sound of high heels as she paced around on the linoleum kitchen floor in a nervous manner.

"I came with the fifty pounds of beans. Could you go out and bring them in?" she said with a heavy Spanish accent. "They're in the trunk."

"Sure thing," Elizabeth said, then came the sound of her opening the door followed by the sound of her struggling with the heavy sack of beans.

"Elizabeth," she said in a sharp tone, "You got to make them last longer. I can't be dropping off fifty pounds more than once per month, I just can't. If you can't make them last longer than this, it'll come out of your twenty. Now, is that clear?" she added, as her pointy heels clicked on the linoleum, and the door slammed shut as an exclamation point. There was a quiet as what the lady had said began to sink in everyone's head.

"Elena, put that back, you're eating way too much," Elizabeth's voice boomed.

"You ain't my boss," Elena countered hotly with the sound of a fridge closing.

"If you don't like the rules here, pack up your stuff, and go live somewhere else," Elizabeth added in an indifferent manner that cut to the heart of the matter.

The next day I felt a lot better and moved back into the garage.

"I better not hear you cough," Elizabeth told me in no uncertain terms who the boss of this place really was. I smiled to myself and nodded.

CHAPTER 15

The Pull of Poetry

I lay down on the bed and watched the day slide by outside as the light went from easy morning to high noon, to a slowly slanting PM. I'd lost track of time and had to struggle to come up with which day it was. My deductive reasoning pinned it down to Thursday, so glancing at my watch, with the light outside getting grey orange, I thought about the poetry night.

Staying at the main house had helped, as my cough now was under control, but the boredom wasn't helping me forget my close brush with the police and how now I had become a person of interest to a paranoid policeman.

I know, I should have stayed in, but the pull was now too great to withstand, so I bundled up and slid the bread bag that held my steno book under my belt. I tried to walk slowly with my hands in my pockets to exert as little as possible. Still, by the time I got to the Alameda Bridge, I had started coughing badly, but I was committed now. I pushed on, wandered up, and opened the door.

The warmth of the coffee house was welcoming, and I found an empty table. As my eyes got accustomed to the dim light, I saw about five or so couples. Norm was over by the wall engrossed in a poem laid in front of him. His head was low, his brow wrinkled, and his shoulders hunched. I watched him, observing a poet, unconscious of my penetrating gaze. He got a relaxed look on his face, after I saw him make changes. I walked up, got a chair, sat down as a coughing spasm hit.

"How are you doing, kid?" he said, looking up from his poem and smiling.

"Not too bad. I'm getting over a cold." I said, coughing, hand to my mouth.

He smiled and said, "You might've spoken too soon. You taking medicine?"

"Nah, I'm going to kick it by myself." I said, looking at his poem on the table. "Got a

good one there?" I asked, holding back a sudden spasm of coughing

"We shall see. Writing them is half the battle. The other half is reading 'um. That's when you see if they have a life of their own or if they're too green. A bunch of words on a sheet of paper does not necessarily a poem make." He added with that contagious smile, as he leaned back and looked around.

I pulled out the bread bag and got out the steno book. Finding my

latest attempt, I read, seeing if the flow would hold.

"What's the deal with this bread bag. You're one of a kind, Cliff. You crack me up you know," he said.

I smiled and saw right behind him the raised stage and mike with a set of lights focused on the stool.

Goldstein

Then came the motion of someone getting up in the flickering shadows. His features came a little at a time—ruffled hair, generic glasses that headed toward the stool. Getting there, he balanced on it. As he sat, his presence radiated tension that caught your eye, telling you that something worth hearing was getting ready to happen. He ruffled through papers, looking at one with intensity. No one wanted to interrupt, even as we waited. Ready, he looked out. "Hello," he said, pushing his glasses back, "I'm David Goldstein. And I've got one I want you to hear. The first one's called *Stillness*."

It's all orange in color or that's how I remember it
The way the tassels of the sawgrass open and spread
Coming up out of the green yellow and brown blades
That against you skin, can cut you like a sharp knife
Or how the rice blades are like so many minnows
That wave in the direction from the current's pull
Like the direction of the wind becoming second nature
Or the patterns you paint with fingers on your face
Which even now for some reason I remember as orange
Learning all the while to be still always in different ways
That whatever you thought it would be before isn't
"No, no, don't hold your breath," that's the first rule
You can lose track of how long under pressure
Maybe faint or you just might move which you can't
Second rule is if you move you're as good as dead
You breathe like the reed moves in the water
One way and then the other never making a ripple
 "Learn from the reed and you just may stay alive"
He would say and then hand me a map and photo
On the map would be an X with a set of coordinates
Nothing else was said except to remember the reed.

You really get to know your heart when you get still
And you learn so much from just listening to it
It is never wrong you find out—not even once
You may think you're doing good everything's fine
And then a little thunder will start deep inside
Enough to let you know that you've left out something
The way your elbows are or how your knees are bent
Cause once it all starts, you can't, not even the slightest
Movement or forgotten detail will give you away
So again, you go back over everything ever so slowly
So you see that you need more mud on your shoes
And you add some dried grass just so and you're okay
You are that reed you keep thinking all the time
Then that click comes into place—the heart evens
There's no voice to tell you but you already know

You know you're okay when a snake comes right by
And you glance at the corner of your eye not moving
And he slides by, you can see the glint in its pupils
Where the light gets pulled in, but he doesn't know
Because he's intent on the prey he's got lined up
He's unaware because you are that reed flowing
It becomes a matter of staying in tune while you wait
Which is the hardest part of all—to keep from moving
So you keep thinking of that reed moving in your mind
And how its strength comes from its ever-firm root
And you see where that flexibility comes from

So you let your mind become that root in place
And you let your heart become that pulling current
Steady and constantly bringing things into view

All the while you, deep inside, know you're all of it
And your trust allows all the rest to fall into place
And then you just wait keeping your eyes out there
Because you know the power of fate is on your side
So when it comes down to that one split-second
The crosshairs line up the features of his face
Or the way his lips will hold their crease just so
Will always be some of the things that stand out
That makes the certainty there a clearer match
So that when the moment gets closer and closer
That the *kerthump, kerthump* kicks in hard
You can feel that surge toward the moment pull

Even before you see his face you can tell it's there
And you know also that he too knows it's coming
In that way there is a compression of expression
And that one part that goes out of sync just a little
So that's the exact moment for the pressure pulling
Everything gets a little tighter a little more tension
All the time with the *kerthump, kerthump* going
Just strong enough so the rhythm matches the beat
Lining up two spots with the third you've memorized
But you don't hold your breath, though you want to
Wanting so bad and you only begin to know why later
Understanding the process, how it's supposed to be
Like that reed, except this time the reed gets cut free
And you watch it slide limp in the current going on
It's then that you notice that it's all turned orange
And that's how you know you find out you don't really.

David stopped and hesitated while we were all transfixed, waiting
for his next flurry of words to weave more of the spell that he had us all

under with his perfect syntax that now allowed the poem to linger in our minds' eyes. He stood for about three or so seconds from the stool. He didn't even wait for the scattered applause that erupted. He just bowed on the way to his table.

The pure ring of his diction gave the words he spoke a life. There was a sheer beauty to the way he enunciated them. It was like you wanted him to take twice as long to enjoy that there really was a certain way that a word was to be said, a certain crystal magic feeling was in the air as he sat down.

I glanced over at Norm and could tell he had noticed too.

My Turn

The *kerthump, kerthump* picked up in tempo and volume. I knew what it meant and walked to the mike, still remembering how well David enunciated his lines so clearly. But poetry is no respecter of persons, and I had to get it out regardless of how I might do in comparison to David—I had to. Before I knew it, I was up on the stage sitting on the stool saying, "I've got one I want to share," and then I started in loudly.

In my eyes streaming with red and white lights
Cars come and go motion with their precious cargo
Everyone with that destination they're heading for
The house with dinner cooking, or the kids to hug
This place that stays just always ahead for me
These decisions that have consequence for me alone
The vagabond in order to keep things free and simple
Like some marrow near the bone that I'm made of
Waiting for these things to stop so I can get a hold
This life that keeps each day to go out of control
Always trying to make it back to where it'll break
But just the same what I end up with are more edges

108

Edges that will turn suddenly without any warning
Thrilling and full of wonder when they come into sight
I just want her there at the end of the day to be
Unasking there supper or her listening ear mine
Which small and bothered that I am will be enough
Upon this wishing star whose light has twinkled weaker
Hold these worded meanings thus fathered to grey
That beginning thus would wind this plea forever
To some sliver of silver light breaking my wishing
To thus of a maybe-to-be that eventual one.

I stopped and allowed a scattering of applause, "Oh, by the way, I'm Cliff Alexander." I added, "Thanks. I've got another one for you that I'd like to read here."

Heavy boots interrupt the night still
Longer moments that won't go away
Like the deer I shot for my first time
Straight up the hill wounded running
That never once as I lined up the sights
Did I see myself running headlong in panic
That part of life that's like this huge wheel
Spinning axis day to day regardless of who
This knot eyes can't see or sharp knives cut
The edges only brain cells will recognize
Which trade off sanity can't abide whole
Because it never stops turning or moving
All the reasons understanding can't fit
Right beside this little voice that says
You gotta keep going, just keep going on.

I stopped stood and looked out over the small audience. This time I saw that only Norm and David were clapping. I walked over and sat down feeling discouraged as I sat down coughing, I looked at David, and he smiled like he was telling me he knew why no one had clapped.

"Not bad," Norm said, winking at me and smiling broadly adding, "We'll talk later, right now I've just got to get up there," he said getting up and heading for the mike, andthere he was alone up there like a grizzly bear retaking his territory by a spawning salmon stream.

Norm's Turn

"Good evening, I'm Norm Moser," he said looking out. "First, let's hear it again for David Goldstein over there," He said, pointing in the direction where David was sitting. David stood,obviously embarrassed. "And, over there, is Cliff Alexander, nice job," he added saying, "Poets feel things that people are afraid to say. I've got one for you that you're going to like," he added, looking down at the paper he had in his hands squinting.

> She was a real doozy, a real wonder
> Never paid no mind to the make-up
> Didn't need to the way some do
> She had her own style like a Rolls
> Some would say more like a Cadillac
> With the top down radio blaring loud
> Feast your eyes, fellas, just don't touch
> Cause if you do, you'd better be ready
> She can be merciless or very kind
> And you never know which way it'll go
> She was a Kmart dresser at heart
> She knew she made the clothes look
> Not vice versa like the avenue ladies
> They say she lost a child a year ago

Only time anyone ever saw her cry
Yes, a Cadillac with plenty of miles
Keeps her oil changed and good tires
Heart of gold good at bending rules
One of a kind one owner and no frills
Get in if you're ready to cut to the chase
Find out fast the lane she'll give you
What you get will be what you deserve
She, like you, knows under it all is a girl
And she'll keep giving til there's no more
Then—she'll find a way to surprise you.

Norm stopped the silence, signaling the poem's ending motionless there on the stage as we waited silent. Then the applause erupted just as spontaneous that brought a broad smile and a nod of acceptance.

Norm had that raw dramatic theater quality to him. He held some of his words or he could sing them out as with this poem so much that you fell under his spell as he spun the lines. You could visualize her there just like a hint of Chanel Number 9 she put on behind her ear that tells you there's so much more. His theatrics allowed you to read between the lines, which, when it ended he went to a frozen stark blank look that still told you, knowing that you were split seconds away from a virtual change of direction or a pivot of subjects that he could dangle you there, eventually giving way enough with that projection so that you still waited curious for what understatement or which new phrase would patch work the next part and hold more. The whole time went hinging on his relentless believability, which his total commitment that made for no other way. In a way, Norm was more of a showman, and his poetry, in many ways, came in a close second, but oddly enough, you'd be wrong too like with his poem about Kathy, who just had to be real, even though there was no sure way of telling for sure. You found that you were witnessing a merging of art and personality of the teller so that they blended together as you sat in awe.

Norm bowed his head and held the pose for a second, then he came down and sat with us like a poet champion. No more grizzly, now back to the earth of his humanity that came by the way he sighed and then looked tired.

David leaned over a table nearby and gave Norm a look. "Thanks," he said, "for the compliment you gave me."

"Which one?" Norm said taking a sip of his herbal tea.

"For calling me a poet," he went on leaning on his chin.

Norm looked at him as he held out his hand to shake, which Norm took and they held the moment then let go. David moved his chair over and looked over at me smiling. "I liked your image of the knot. Not half bad." He added holding out his hand like he'd done with Norm just before. We both shook hands like two young bullfighters meeting after going the full distance against a huge thrusting beast.

"How do you speak the way you do?" I asked, wanting to know. He got an awkward look on his face, and looked at the mike. "Golly," I added, "you could do Shakespeare with your diction."

"Well, I've played in his plays but I decided to change from being an actor to a poet since you put more on the line." He said leaning back in his chair.

Norm was nodding his head as he listened to our conversation. "Yes," he interjected, "your diction is one of your strengths."

"I'm worried that it will get in the way of what I trying to say," David said to our surprise, our combined looks witnessed.

112

I couldn't believe what I heard. "Are you kidding?" I said.

Norm interrupted saying, "I know what you mean, and, that's spoken as a true poet too, I might add, you'd think we were crazy or something the way we think. Cliff, it's the same with your images. They are so well placed that they speak for you in spite of your lack of expression. The images stay on and do the talking enriching the meanings. If a poet was in a shipwreck and had to choose which one he'd go overboard with—either his poems or his life jacket, he'd find himself having to stop for a moment to decide which. Some would take the poems and some would the jacket. We are, for certain, a crazy bunch of outsider social rejects."

While Norm spoke, both of us nodded freely our agreement. I put my hand to my mouth and a spasm of coughing erupted, which I tried to hold back not wanting to miss his dialogue since he was speaking for each one of us, as we huddled there as if in a safe harbor, feeling this strength Norm was sharing.

"Oh yes," Norm added, taking a sip of his cup of tea, "ah, Cliff, you expected a lot from that second poem you read but," he stopped, looked around, "It was a poet's poem, that means it wasn't for everyone, and some didn't stay with it. But, then, that's the way it goes. Sure, work on your delivery; you say the lines without that zing that comes from your gut. Poems are like French cooking, you gotta take time to enjoy it, and when you hurry a line that you don't trust, you don't let that connection happen and it all gets lost there. A poem has a life of its own that the listener gets hooked into. You've got to trust that it's there, and to believe it, to pull it off.

"David here, has a classical pure resonant delivery, that in itself, holds the listener to the sheer power words have on their own and that dynamic holds the listener to just what is getting said. Me, on the other hand, I have that look out below, here-I-come way of taking the poem

113

on the roller coaster that it takes me believing in my emotions, and that's where my power resides."

Norm took another sip of his tea and swallowed looking at us as we sat there, nodding at what he was saying like apt pupils. He went on. "Bottom line is that tonight people will go home, and each one will think and wonder about your waving reed and how life goes on in spite of the knives out there that's cut, and when they hear the name Kathy, they'll think about—"

"A yellow Cadillac," David and I chimed in smiling at each other. "And guess what?" he said, looking at us, "We're worth our salt." With that he stood and stretched and took a last sip of his tea. "Well, I gotta go," he said looking at us, "tonight was good."

As he left, we both said, "See you later, Norm. Take good care."

It got quiet a while, as we sat there and thought about his ideas. "So, when did you serve in Vietnam?" I asked him out of the blue. David sighed, glanced away. "A long time ago and far, far away."

"You serve?" he asked me after a while, looking out into space.

"Yeah, I got drafted but would not accept the gun on principle, ended up being a medic, then got orders to Vietnam and decided it was time to take a stand that I would not be part of their war, so I ended up in the stockade for disobeying this lawful order. The stockade messed me up good," I said, looking out the window at the way the wind was blowing, twisting a tree limb as the leafless branch was hefted one way and then another.

"It took a lot of guts to take a stand like that," he said finally. "It was one of those lonely deals when you'll be all by yourself."

"What'a you mean," I interrupted, "you're the one with the guts, going out like you did with just a map with an X and a photo. Golly, I don't know what I'd a done with an assignment like that."

"You're a good listener," he said. "Most people don't hear that; they get caught up in the image of the snake and don't go on."

It got quiet for about ten minutes or so of silence, looking around as different people came in and sat down and began conversing. "The color orange was a nice contrast to the poem," I said. "It was like it didn't belong, yet it did on an emotional level."

"You know what I think? We both got knots inside thanks to the Army. Well, I gotta go," he said, rising to leave.

We shook hands with a solid handshake. "See you, David," I said, looking at him, returning his gaze.

"Take care of your cough," David said smiling, then he was gone.

CHAPTER 16

Staying Power

Dad's Visit

Going to the poetry night had ended up really costing me a lot, as my cold relapsed and my coughing was becoming incessant. The week prior, I had received a letter from Dad letting me know he was going to come by to visit; so that hesitant knock on my door was no surprise. I opened the door trying to hold back my reflex to start coughing. We hugged and held each other longer than I remember. The water of my stockade lockup had passed since we'd meet last. He glanced with a father's eye at my mattress lying on the floor.

I smiled as if nothing was amiss, adding, "I'm getting my bearings." I saw that awkward motion, the hesitant silence, his deep sigh. He never was good at faking it or at small talk, so he said, "You hungry? Is there someplace close by that we could go and get something?"

"There's a Furr's Cafeteria just down the road at a small mall," I said, putting my shoes on adding, "this costs me sixty a month, not too bad, huh?" I said with a note of pride thinking back to that day I went looking and had found this diamond in the rough.

I followed him out to his rental car, got in and we headed out. He took a left on St. Michael's, going south to the shopping mall. I got the macaroni and the spice loaf of bread with peas and ice tea. Dad kept saying when we went by the roast beef section of the line, "Come on, get some meat," with a good-natured push in his voice.

"Nah thanks," I responded, "I'm trying to keep it as simple as I can, as I put a pat of butter on my tray that I wouldn't have normally. We sat down near the line of windows said grace and started eating. He was just like I had remembered him with his humble manner, unassuming in both his presence and that quiet air about him.

You wouldn't have guessed this same man flew planes off carriers during the Second World War and faced death each day of his life. Flying those airplanes was why he had a plan for everything, and I couldn't help but feel that I had missed out on some of his genes. He brought his own silent cadence to life and with this awkwardness of silence that he felt no compunction of filling as we both ate our meals, as if this was just a regular meal at the end of a usual day.

He had something to tell me that he wasn't sure how I was going to take it, by the way he was eating his meal like a cab driver in traffic, with his eye checking the rear view as he waited for an opening to make his move. As he ate, there was a prolonged humbleness to his movements, as if he was saying that he was sorry for not being with me while I was doing time in the stockade for following my conscience. Maybe, he felt the conflict I felt had come from his nurturing my following my conscience, which had lead me to disobey that order. That was a stretch, but it would have been a correct one.

He showed noticeable vulnerability as he cut his meat. He took a deep sigh and I thought, look out, here it comes. "Have you tried to get on as a lab tech and use your education? With your qualifications, you should be able to make good money. You could do better than you are now as," he hesitated a second since he well knew he was heading toward troubled waters.

"A dishwasher," I interrupted, "you don't understand, I can't," I stammered, actually afraid of what truth might come out then. "I need space right now, I'm," I said, looking straight into his eyes, which caught him off-guard so that he got sad and gazed out the window at a distant object.

In a lot of ways, I was that open raw nerve with a thin veneer, so the conversation shifted to generalities that went back and forth that spoke of a kinship as much as an emotional distance.

Here was this son in deep water, determined to get out of a riptide on his own. Each question lead to another unanswered question, on and on, that in my mind, spoke more of the joy of the search then of gaps, so after a while with the meal ended, we drove over to the square.

As we got there, a parade of colors erupted in the western sky with the colors going from orange to lavender to a combination so that I felt the pull, felt that I wanted to sit and let the show evolve just above me, but Dad was too impatient to let the colors work inside of him, so we wandered back to his car and sat outside the library.

As our conversation waned, I could feel the sunset pulling on me so much that my mind wandered off of exactly what it was that we were talking about.

Out of the blue he said, "But son, you are going nowhere out here. Can't you see that you can do much better than washing dishes?" Another father would have glossed it over with smooth innuendos, but not Dad. He was always damn-the-torpedoes, full-speed-ahead, a bull-in-the-psyche china shop, making things to fall out simply and direct.

I could feel the pressure so I couldn't come up with words. "I gotta go, Dad," I said, still feeling the pull of that sunset working. I reached for the door handle and pulled on it, tripping the levers.

"Wait, son," Dad's voice went to a level that I'd never heard before. But I was determined to pull harder on the handle. "Please don't go," he pleaded in a voice that fell on my deaf ears as I was not going to be manipulated by his emotion right then.

I just knew I had to get out of there, so I left him alone just like that. The sunset was now a dim lavender going to a crystal-clear gray. My breath puffed out a cloud of gray, signaling winter's silent onset. This freedom thing was all I had—that and my sight into the beauty. Prior to right now, I was always on someone else's tight schedule. I cooled down and worked my way to Cerrillos Road to Dad's motel that he had pointed out. This time I knocked at the door and waited nervously.

"Come on in," he said, opening it up as if he had been expecting me.

"Sorry, Dad," I began, "but right now I'm doing the best that I can."

The sad look in his face, along with his inability the fake it, told me that I'd fallen below expectations, which was why I was here in the first place. A conversation would have gone nowhere, which was why I said nothing else. I coughed some, trying to hold back the spasm waiting to happen.

"How long have you had that cough?" he asked, sitting on the bed.

"About two weeks. I was getting better but got out too early and I relapsed," I answered, sitting in the easy chair by the window.

"Hey, if you want, you could stay here in that extra bed over there, and take a nice long hot shower too. There's plenty of hot water," he added, getting up and getting something out of his suitcase.

"I gotta work tomorrow, but if you could drop me off, then okay that sounds good.

It's been a while since I had a long hot shower."

"No problem, I could drop you off on my way out of town," he said.

I took that shower and felt the heat work its way into my muscles. I thought about the commune and my near interlude with Susan, and I thought about her and wondered where she might be right now, along with the thoughts of Norm and David, as the water ran over my body and my cough reflex relaxed a bit.

When I got out and dried off, Dad was on the bed reading the Bible and had the TV. "Should be the first good snowstorm of the year," the weatherman said. Dad woke me up to get to the restaurant right at seven. Pulling over in front of the place, he leaned over to give me a hug. I felt the stiff hard stubble of his cheek whiskers he had missed—one of his constants from way-back memories floating in the now that came as a sudden glimpse, as I opened the door to get out.

"Oh," he added, pushing forty dollars in my hand before I turned around, adding, "you better see a doctor about that cough and get medicine." And then, his white Chevy Nova, with the Hertz tag on the back, headed south in the early hazy morning light toward Albuquerque. Just like that, I was standing alone in front of the restaurant with this gnawing inside, that let me know I wasn't out of the woods, which scared me so but at the same time gave meaning to my steps as I headed in to face the morning breakfast rush, full force on my own.

Going to the Clinic

Jan went with me to see the doctor and waited in the office patiently, while I took deep breaths and coughed and repeated again while the doctor listened with his stethoscope, moving it here and there. I let out my breaths slowly to a wheezing sound, trying not to cough. He wrote down his prescription, and I paid him fifteen of the forty. The medicine cost an additional ten so with fifteen dollars, Jan and I went to the Chinese Restaurant west on San Francisco.

"Thanks for coming with me," I said, looking at her long hair that was still frizzed with static from running a comb through it.

I could feel the medicine kicking in, as the wheezing was easing and my urge to cough was becoming less and less, almost gone.

The waitress brought the white rice that steamed up in front. I could see through the cloud that Jan had on a snug sweater. I saw her smile, as if she was reading my mind as I glanced away over to the painting they had on the back wall of an orange sun just behind her.

We enjoyed our meal and ended up over at her place to talk more. The one small bulb in the corner of her apartment softened the light. I reached out and ran my fingers gently through her long dark hair, parting a snag and continuing on to the next one saying not a word. She closed her eyes and leaned toward me.

Our lips brushed almost accidently at first, then with more intensity. I saw snatches of her closed eyes, the way her hair fell across her shoulders, and then our touch became like eyes of their own and knew what to do before they came to that place.

I fell into that relativity that spun silk soft beneath my hand can create, so that night we went to this place that we never had experienced, out into the deepest part of our dreams. We swam out into the breakers where we drowned til sleep quenched our thirst with its deep black.

CHAPTER 17

One of Those Days

I rested up the whole weekend at my place, and by Monday morning was feeling much better. Out the window, sure enough, large white flakes were floating down. The weatherman had gotten it right. The sky was a deep grey with a slight touch of a breeze that put an angle to feathered flight of the flakes that were already piling up on the ground.

I got dressed and put on my warm coat and my rainbow-colored, knit skull-cap, and I headed toward town as cars crunched on the snow going slow. The medicine had done the trick and my health was back full. With great gusto, I pushed my way enjoying the elements and how stark the way the wind was working patterns ahead of the swirling eddies that evened out and disappeared to the ground. There was so much paradox in one event that made me smile thinking about it, completely free to take what was going on and to see into it—not to stay on the surface of the cold but to see this beauty that was going on around me. My hands were stuffed into my pockets, my collar up, my head down, crossing the railroad tracks, heading northeast for the buildings whose darker shadows I caught a glimpse of now and then.

Rude Awakening

It was too early to hit the library, so I changed my route and took Alameda and went east where I could see the city open up toward the north. Taking a turn, I headed down a narrow alley behind some stores. I could see a car heading in my direction so I got off to the side with my head down so I did not see the pothole come up in front, which unlucky coincidence brought us there at the same time. When the tires slammed down sending the slush upward, I was in exactly the wrong spot. This wave came full force as I looked up from my position and could see it was coming at me—a whole wave of frozen slush that hit me broadside drenching me. When it hit me, it took my breath away, waking me up from what reverie I had been in—in a rude extreme manner. Just like that, I had this instantaneous hypothermic realization that led to a spontaneous direction change toward The La Fonda Hotel where in my mind I could see that fireplace even before I got there.

Sure enough, the logs were already burning licking orange, as I sat down. I took solace knowing that I had friends on the staff, which would cut me slack, looking the way I did soaking wet. I got in the chair that was closest to the spark-cracking flames and sat with my hands toward the infrared that was coming off, as the flames cracked and sputtered in the adobe-lined hearth.

The flames were filling in the crevices of the jagged rough logs, as the embers gave off purple hues along with the usual deep red, while the inner coals glowed and vibrated red with a shade of violet. Near all this heat radiating out, my shivering subsided and my compulsion to shake all over gave, a little at a time, away.

Pablo, the guy I had helped at the ER, came by and nodded at me, and with that, I relaxed more and got into the motion of the fire seeing how the color would dance outside of the orange and burn higher, then disappear as the energy long ago stored was released in the middle of my plight. I could see the cycles were meshing that sent me pondering about a mix of a greater order as I sat there now completely warm and dry, seeing concentric rings expanding as if that accident had been really a pebble thrown into a pond ever-widening sub-universes, with me here in a corner getting replenished.

A spark crackled and flew out in front of me, pulsing red and violet. Then it went to an ashen gray with a slight plume of smoke that went up and disappeared. Wide or narrow, the ringed story of the years of this tree was telling unfolded before me—its good and lean years that were being unleashed down to the last molecule that had been woven by a leaf into the loom of its trunk.

As the changes went on in front of me in the fireplace crackling, I was beginning to catch on past my anger to listen and be still. I glanced at the clock over on the wall, which read eleven-fifteen, which meant that the library would now be open for business. As I walked down the hall, I saw Pedro and gave him a wave. He smiled and waved back. It was good to have a friend here. Heading past the magazines of the smoke shop, I walked, hands in my pockets, back out into the snowstorm that was going already leaving six inches on the sidewalk and slush in the streets.

I crossed the street, walked under the store awnings, flake free, across the intersection glancing down the Palace of Governors and the sheltered sidewalks where the Indians displayed wares on blankets with the owners staring out towards the square at the people passing right on. It was cold but you couldn't tell by looking at their still silhouettes with their blankets wrapped around them. It was too cold for me to wander on by, so I took a detour and glanced at the different styles of workmanship in a hurried manner.

An Indian guy approached me who wore a funny pie-shaped hat colored iris, with a triangle of a darker brown inset of an amber color. He held out some pinon nuts, and I took three and looked back at him.

He made a motion as if I should pop them into my mouth, which I did. I bit down hard, and as I did the shell collapsed under my pressure, and I spit out the mucus-mixed mess of nut and shell to his enjoyment.

"No, no," he said, putting one in his mouth and biting on it sideways so that it was more on his incisors, and he rolled it with his tongue and spit out the two pieces of brown shells and held out his tongue. On it was a cream-colored fleshy nut, that he proceeded to chew up. He smiled and motioned for me to try again, which I did, trying harder not to crunch down so on the shell, but to no avail as it gave way and I had a mass of nut and shell again, which I spit out in front of me.

By now, the whole line of Indians behind their blankets were all smiling and getting a kick out of my chewing, so I tried harder with another one but the shell still gave way. By now they were laughing, so I retreated and shrugged and went back to my original destination. I took that left turn at the end of the Governors Palace walkway to the library, up the long brick steps. The bulletin board was crowded with ads: bikes for sale, roommates wanted, skis for sale real cheap, rides wanted, where everyone was trying to find what they wanted or what they had to offer without paying the newspaper.

Yes, It Can

At the magazine rack that had *New Yorker* and *People* magazines, I grabbed like a hungry dog and found an empty seat. An article about The Who intrigued me. It was in depth, about whether lifestyle dictated music or vice versa. The author was passing up the obvious for the sake of the mundane that had a more intellectual slant so that he could make his point.

In the corner of my eye a young lady had moved into my peripheral view. There was a Sophia Loren likeness to her eyes with the same oval shape, along with deep brown color that immediately interrupted my train of thought.

"Excuse me," she said reaching for the *People* magazine beside me, "may I read it until you're done with the *New Yorker*?" She hesitated a moment, and then reached over.

"Go right ahead, help yourself," I said, glancing over at her.

She smiled, saying, "Thanks," and took off her serape her serape that still had white snowflakes attached to the fabric. Her beauty was so natural and unaffected, that I was taken by surprise. I smiled and returned to my magazine about The Who. My field of vision included her face across from me. Her cheeks were still a rich ruddy red color from the cold outside. The problem with her eyes was that I kept wanting to stare at them, but I fought the desire and turned another page, scanning photos instead.

I could hear her still breathing deeply from the exertion of her walk. I allowed her face to come into full view as I glanced as if I was looking behind her outside the window at the snow that was still floating down out of the deep grey mysterious sky. We made full eye contact and I tried to manage an awkward smile, not wanting to give away the fact that I was in way over my head.

Golly, her eyes are just beautiful, I thought over and over to myself. She held her stare long enough for me to evoke a safe response. I only hoped that what came out of my mouth would make sense. She beat me to it by saying, "Didn't you used work at the ER last summer?"

"Yes, but I got fired for lack of discretion," I said, happy I hadn't messed up.

"You remember that little girl that got hurt at the Zozobra Parade? ah," she went on, "she got her leg pinched badly by a semi-trailer."

I nodded, remembering what seemed a long time ago. "Yes," I said, thinking back to that evening afterward walking to the commune.

"She's my cousin. My uncle thinks highly of you. You were the one that really helped her," she added. "He says that you were more help than all the doctors were that day."

I could feel my face flushing as she was touching a still-soft part. I could still see the girl biting on her lower lip, holding back the pain, with her breathing that came sometimes in a rush.

"She sure had a lot of courage, for such a little girl," adding, "How is she now?"

"She's got a limp. It's the scar tissue, the doctors say," she said.

"I'm really happy for her. She was a real trooper, no quit in her."

"What are you doing now?" she asked, glancing to her magazine. She looked up,

catching me gazing at her beautiful face and she blushed.

My mind went blank with all these options suddenly opening. I felt like pinching myself to be sure this was really happening and found myself saying, "I'm working out on Cerrillos at the Pantry Restaurant."

"Oh," she responded. Her eyes went to a place where she was thinking back herself, adding,

"After that I'm thinking that I'll go into nursing. Funny, how before that accident, I hadn't given it a thought, but after visiting her and watching her improve, slowly, I got pulled in. Seeing what she went through, and seeing where she's at now, something took a good hold inside of me."

"Helping others can get under your skin," I added. "Funny, what it takes, for us to find out about ourselves." Suddenly, I could feel currents of doubt pulling hard inside of me. I wanted the connection to stay, but I felt it was sliding out of sight so I went back to *The New Yorker* and held on for all that I was worth. The article was about victims of war. I tried hard to get into the flow, but her beauty was too much. Her cheeks were full of youth with a rosy hint. All that my peripheral vision would allow I took, as I turned a page. Her lips had a fullness as she smiled at something that she had just read.

So many things were turning inside of me at once. It was hard to not screw this up. If not for her, I would have had to go for a walk to get a grip, but I didn't want to lose out on what might happen. *Crap*, I thought. We both turned to the end of our magazines at the same time.

"Well," she said, "you can have the *People* magazine, I'm done," she said, reaching over for her serape and glancing at the clock.

My moment of truth was upon me as my ideas were scrambling. "Ah," I said hoping this would be good, "I feel like a walk too," I added quickly. "Would you mind if I braved the storm with you?" Out the window the flakes were still fluttering down.

"Ah," she stopped and thought, her beautiful face now pensive. "No, I don't mind at all," she said, slipping on her alpaca serape.

I took a deep breath (proud of myself) and put up the magazines. I watched her hair flow over the designs of the serape and curl over. She turned to see if I was coming. I smiled my one-front-tooth smile, and we went down the steps and into the quiet of the flakes that covered the top of her head, showing pure white. I put on my rainbow-colored cap from a thrift store. We crossed the street, weaving between cars as they crunched with their treads gripping the fresh snow. We trudged through eight inches of snow, stepping high, until we got to the veranda of the shops.

Rivulets were running from the roof gutter along the building's corner. We slowed and glanced at the display laid out on a velvet cloth. The quality was much finer than the Indian vendors by the Governors Palace. I couldn't help noticing under her serape the curves of a grown woman. We crossed the street and went by Walgreens and down San Francisco, going in and out of the spiraling flakes coming out of the grey sky. I could tell there was a hesitation for her to stay with me and me her. We turned and went into a clothing store where she found a sweater that she liked and she held in front of her and laughed as she posed.

I whistled and raised my eyebrows *ala* Groucho Marx and laughed. There was a simpleness to her that told of an innocent zest for life, along with those hazel eyes and rosy cheeks and her white teeth. This could be a dream, except my feet were wet and cold.

Then we headed back out and continued west toward the barrios where small stucco houses spumed smoke from their chimneys. We walked quietly for a while, crossing streets and jumping puddles until we came to a gravel driveway that lead to a stucco house. There she stopped and looked at me saying, "Thanks for walking me home." She hesitated, and then turned and headed slowly toward the house. Suddenly she stopped, turned, "Oh, I'm Gabriel, Gabriel Lopez." And then just like that, she walked to the doorway and disappeared.

I was left standing there with the smell of her perfume on my mind that lingered along with the soft way she had said her name Gabriel, which echoed in my head and wove with the memory of that scent that in my mind conjured images of lace and whispers and candles.

130

I became aware of the cold breeze that rattled the pods of Acacia trees, and I retraced my steps in the dry snow back toward town. As I got to the next street, a group of guys suddenly appeared behind an adobe wall that fronted the sidewalk.

"Hey, gringo, *que está*? You lost or something?" the bigger one said. I turned to see a Spanish guy standing in front. As we traded looks, this group slowly surrounded me, leaving no exit. My first impulse was to run, but I stayed put and tried to look cool.

The one guy got closer saying, "Yes, *ese*, I think you like Gabrielle." He reached out, touched my face, "What's wrong with white skin?"

I pushed his hand away and stepped back ready for what was next.

"Oh, so you're pretty tough, *ese*?" he said, squaring his shoulders.

"I don't want no trouble," I said, stepping toward the street.

His two buddies got in the way so that I had to stop.

"Let him go, I'm smelling yellow, and I don't want to get that on me," he said. "But gringo, next time you come this way, you're gotta pay bad." The two guys parted and I headed toward town.

I could feel my heart thumping, as I crossed the street in the snow. As I got closer to town, I was able to gain my wits. When I got to the square, I found a park bench and settled in, thinking how unexpected, but real, the incident I'd been able to escape had been. *What a close call*, I said to myself, still thinking about Gabriel and her gentle impression. Even in the face of what I'd just been through, I felt clear about—those oval eyes, and that texture of her skin on her face and neck.

What a junky circumstance, I admitted, but which I had to let go of, so I spaced it out. For now, I'd stay away and play it safe. I allowed myself to get into the flow of the park with the motions of cars, people, and animals in constant flux. I noticed one scruffy dog and stayed with his routine as he went to one trash can, then another, jumping up and sniffing, taking a good whiff of the can to test its contents. When the terrier found one to his liking, he'd check around, then leap in, only to remerge, with the remnants of a hamburger in his chops.

A larger dog noticed this, and tried to intimidate him, but the terrier quickly scanned the vehicles of the oncoming traffic. After allowing the larger dog to get near him, he stepped in the lane. With the dog intent on his prize, he failed to see the oncoming truck whose bumper was too high for the terrier, but just right to hit the larger dog, throwing it completely out of balance. It yelped, retreating as the terrier trotted in front of the truck, then across the street, only to disappear down an alley that was running with snowmelt.

I watched the whole scenario unravel in front of me on the bench. For now, I'll be like that terrier and make use of my circumstances and trust my wits to figure out a workable scenario when the time comes. With that thought intact, I gazed at the blue sky that was radiating down rays that made the snow go heavy and begin to run into the trickling gutters.

CHAPTER 18

This Current that Was Me

I didn't know if it was just me or if the poems themselves had a life that were dying to get told and to take shape to a live audience; or whether the people's expectation made the air electric, flickering candles.

Some came in two by two, sometimes a single person, sitting alone. The days were getting shorter and the darkness was falling earlier. People were reacting to cold weather, wanting to come together. Silhouettes were alive on the wall as people talked animatedly, and their conversations rose and fell with the excitement, when a new idea engendered in both parties. I felt that spontaneity was about to happen. Rabbits were going to be pulled out of the metaphors that the poems were going to reveal.

The poems that were in my steno book had promise, as I had been taking the creative process less and less for granted. For the first time, I spent time working them over. The labor had created an edgy feeling that I was on the line and there was no way that I was going to talk myself out of reading them to see if that life flow was there or not.

Norm had come in and had gone in the back room to get tea. He came out, and I could tell from how he glanced, that he was ready. He gave me a nod of recognition and took off his coat, then sat down on the stool. He pulled sheets from his folder and looked at them much as Picasso would one of his paintings, with a long lean look not wanting to give away that they were ready to explode, just like he was a poker player holding a good hand. He took a deep breath like he was getting ready to take a deep dive.

We both sat there like boxers waiting to get it on with our take on life, knowing that, in a while, it would be time and the flow would start. He took a sip of his tea and took a longer look at a certain poem.

David Goldstein came in with a beautiful blonde on his arm and sat at a table right near us, giving us a look, a nod, then looked around. The lady had on a dark brown down vest and a turtleneck under it. She had that beauty that wasn't drop-dead gorgeous but nearly so, only that she had an unkempt look to her that said she was beyond it. She whispered to him, glanced around, and laughed at a private joke, that they both seemed to get at the same time. I could tell by the way he was clutching his stack of papers there that he was as amped as we were, only, he was the king of diction and I was the lisper, only as good as the way my images made magic.

Norm ambled over to the mike, "Testing, testing, good evening, poetry lovers. Welcome to the Mt. Ararat Coffee House. I'd like to kick off this poetry night with one of my own." He glanced away and stood still, regaining his bearing on the poem as his expression totally changed and with it, the mood of the room. This serious mood came over him, unlike what we'd been used to. "It's called *You're Still Here*," he said, clearing his throat.

You're still there while I stir my tea
The steam is rolling over the cup's lip

Just like you not to make a big deal
By the way you sit there saying nothing
With your arms folded looking outside
As the wind tosses the leaves in the air
While I wish that you'd scream out at me
Throw something at me or take my head off
That makes this hard stone cold in my throat
Worse and it seems to be stronger than I
Words stuck sideways not making it out
But you know well how the silence talks
So in a way we are having a conversation
About cutting this bone out of my side
But you won't move from your place
So much like that child I keep on seeing
That I just can't though I want to real bad
Watching with you at the swirling leaves
Knowing that not wanting to see won't work
At making it all go away like it did before
Skipping back to what was once so good
Like ignoring this sound deep in my throat
Making me say it as simply as it can get said
But you won't look at me there struggling
I gotta go for a walk is what comes out instead
We both know how the razors work innocently
When they're turning sideways inside of my gut
And I know that all the walks won't make it undo
But I'm still going out the door into the dark night
My collar up and my hands deep in my pockets
And I still know that even after some long steps
Up around the mesa and down the gulley's back
That you'll still be there looking over the view
Out the window waiting for what I can't do

This storm that won't stop raging inside of me
As I leave this other one outside blowing hard.

He stopped and looked out into the quiet of the room and you could have heard a pin drop in the utter silence. He bowed his head, signaling the poem was over. The applause came but more subdued, almost hushed.

To me it was hard seeing Norm like this—more human, rather that spouting words about a car-hop teenager. He always seemed on top of everything, spinning a tale or coming around the bend with just the right control. Now he had struggled with what he was trying to say. He walked over, sat down exhausted, and took a sigh of relief, as if he was hoping that by saying those words he may have exercised some demon. I didn't know what to say, so I kept my mouth shut and waited.

David glanced at his companion, then headed to the mike. His broad smile was an unmistakable addition to his countenance. As he came closer to the stool, he ran his fingers in his curly hair. He coughed, adjusted to mike, and pushed his glasses back, "I've got one for you called *Yvonne's Net.*" He spoke much as a musician does to find his pitch, with his voice striking a deeper tone with some words. You could tell, as people stopped conversing and hushed their own voices, that there was a certain commanding quality, that clear pitch brings. As he cleared his throat, his remarkable voice had a power that held us.

David's Poem

Rosanne in the night light suspended
This is me going down out of sight
Disappearing into your embraced night
With the stars blinking over your shoulder
Why I can't even start to ask what it is
That I want so bad I can hardly take it

How it is that you know exactly what it is
The part of me that I never had before
Painting my soul behind your smile
How you don't even seem to care one way
Or another how much you really own me
That in your breath I feel the stars move
Their orbits sliding past all my wishes
Light years away yet still in the middle
Were this touch the start of another Orion
Just past your glance into my kindled aurora
Climbing sighs with wings of fire and glass.

David stopped and looked motionless for a split second, bowed and then nodded at the audience, signaling the poem was over. As the applause started, he bowed again, then left the stage and walked back to the pretty blonde. I glanced at her closer. There was just something about her, that as she sat there, unimpressive in her demeanor that reminded me of a city girl adept at matters of the heart. There was a polished way beneath that rough cover.

David's rich resonant voice was hard to follow, but I had no choice as my heart had already kicked up a beat, and wouldn't let go like I had this giant gyroscope spinning fast inside of my chest. I just had to uncoil it as I unfolded the piece of paper and my rendezvous with words. Here goes, as I looked around, moving on, and started for the mike. All of a sudden it was gone. That feeling burning red hot left me halfway to the mike, but I was committed so I played it cool as if I really had something I had to get out. I went up to the mike and adjusted it, looking out as I did.

"I've got one I want to share, it's called *Armed with a Pencil*," I said, taking a deep breath as if I was ready for a deep dive, a free dive without an aqua lung, out into the deep water, here goes, zeroing on the words and feeling the pull start.

> Armed with a pencil and a pressing need
> Which thrones me to write of the watchful heart
> Sight blazing behind words straining the pitch
> To rend through the fever to life's gentle blend
> Balanced to the poet's eye simple ways fall
> Together in their searching bounding pulse
> Winding aside casted darkness groping at times
> Alone, in solitude's sanctum for a light in it all
> If faintly first whispering free there struggling
> To gather into these words its illusive frailty
> Burning new beside your threading heart
> And as my silent stones each break apart
> Their thrashing shall ring in the sky like a dove.

I stopped and looked out at the audience that seemed rapt, as if the words must have hit chords in them. For the first time, I felt that bond go beyond me to them—the power of the words had evoked all by themselves, since my style was simple at best. Norm's applause was way above the rest in its enthusiasm, but I sat down. He didn't have anything to say to me, which made me think that the poem must have touched something. As the applause died down, I could tell it wasn't for me at all, but for what the words had done with their weave and magic. It took me by surprise, so I tried to seem like it was no big deal. Other poets read poetry from cummings; another did one by T.S. Eliot which was really pretty good. But for me, the diamonds had come from David, Norm, and me.

Norm glanced over at me and gave a nod, stood still in that somber mood. I nodded back and passed David's table on my way.

"Nice poem," I said, glancing at David. I noticed the blonde's hand around his. On the crease just above her thumb was a tattoo of a heart with an arrow through it. "See you next Thursday," I added.

"Not if I see you first," he added, smiling.

Norm had left without saying a word, which as I thought about it on my way back to my apartment was worth more to me, than had he had gone on with positives. As I went by the light posts and the leafless limbs that reached up under the moon that was a crescent slice midst a stream of stars and thought that my poetry was coming along.

CHAPTER 19

Finding David's Place

The next day I dressed and went for a walk in the cold. The snow was spotty, about half melted due to the sun's light. When the afternoon got above freezing, especially in the spots, direct rays could work uninterrupted. Behind trees or on the shady north side of the buildings, the snow showed, though it had a gray crust of cinders. I headed around an arroyo east of town up a worn-out county road.

I walked among cedars and pine trees on the contoured hills. The sound of *caw, caw, caw* came from the top of a fence-post perch. A raven narrated my presence to any animals in the area—nature's ever vigilant connoisseur of fresh remains or roadkill, the roving recyclers in feathers with their flinty beaks, and glinty eyes. Their heads that kept changing the angles of their weary perception.

Right behind the raven, I noticed smoke rolling out of a chimney of an adobe house that came sharply into focus, visible beside the partially melted dirty drifts. The smoke curled up grey as if it had found a hole in the sky's belly. I was still out of breath from the previous slope I had climbed up, so I sat down on dry ground on the humped side of this hill beside where the road wound its way through the dots of cedar and pinon eastward. I lay down, looked up, and let the ground's warmth travel to my body. I looked at the adobe house with its flat roof and deep-set windows.

Just then, someone came out and walked slowly over to the wood pile. He got the axe stuck in a log and started chopping. The splintering noise was a split second behind the swinging motion as the wood flew apart, only later came the clatter of the wood chips. Something about the guy chopping looked familiar. He looked like David or maybe was someone that looked a lot like him. I squinted looking closer at him and noticed the same ruffled curly hair.

"Hey," I yelled over, expecting him to recognize my voice right off. He glanced in my direction, taking a long look, also squinting as he did. I felt awkward about the time he was taking to respond, so I waved and walked toward him. As I got closer, I could tell he recognized from how his face relaxed.

"Hey, Cliff, I recognized your one-of-a-kind voice," he said.

"No problem," I said, holding out my hand, adding, "I was out on a walk, stopped to rest over there, and saw you."

"Come on in, it's a little cold out here to talk," he motioned me to come in. I grabbed firewood to carry in with me and followed him in dropping the wood on the pile beside the stove.

"Here sit," he said, sliding a chair over from a table toward me. "I'll make hot cocoa. What'a you out so early for?"

"Oh, I have this thing about four walls that I just can't take," I said. "Nice place you've got here." The furnishings were sparse at best, but functional at the same time. A rocking chair was beside the fireplace, and over by the window was the table and cook stove and a cupboard with cans of chili, soup, and a sack of rice. On another table was a radio.

141

It had the man's touch, it was easy to tell, as piles of stuff were all over. Over by his bed dirty clothes were piled up; on a desk on the other side of the window were piles of papers.

"Here," he said, sliding a cup of cocoa on the table. "So, you can't take boredom very well."

"No, I'm not good at whiling away the time unless I'm doing something. I'm like what they say about sharks: they have to keep moving to keep water filtering through their gills to stay alive."

He glanced at my neck. "I don't see any gills," he glanced at my bag hanging on the back of my belt that had my steno notebook and smiled.

"You and your bag. You have your own style, Cliff, I gotta say that." He added, "By the way I liked that poem you read at the last reading."

"Thanks," I said, "the response really surprised me."

"Every now and then we get lucky, like a miner finding that vein that everyone relates to, and the words become keys to our locks."

I pulled out my steno book from the bag and laid it on the table. "Got any ones in there you would like to share?" he asked.

I smiled and thumbed through the pages looking for this one and finding it. "Just so happens that I do," I said. "Here you go, I call it *Andrea's Way.*"

Biting her lips was the way to hold it back
Not saying how much it hurt also helped
But the way the wound looked on her leg
With the jagged edges of flesh opened up
No telling how many nerves were crushed

Or how she could even smile at my questions
And nod her head with expression to say yes
Like she was on the edge of a high building
Not knowing all the time how far down it was
That I could tell could happen at any moment
So I kept her busy with my questions and talk
As the serious doctors in the back conferred
Looking at the X-rays mumbling in low tones
As they talked about the possible amputation
But you could tell somewhere in the back
Of her eyes in the look that searched deeply
That it was there—that ungiving-up squint
This child as she took another breath held it
And let it out between clenched teeth tight lips
As she listened to my answers reassuring her
Yes, she was going to be okay, yes, I was sure
She had dreams that were needing to happen
That could not be broken so young, not even
So I stayed there beside her that thin time
A stranger whose love of dreams was pure
Which was all he himself had to believe in
And could not let any other thought to sway
Andrea what part of you was me right then
And what part am I in you right this minute
That either of us would give all that we are
For them to be true why I could not lie to you.

David sat there, stroking his chin slowly as I read the lines.
"Beautiful, beautiful," he said, getting up and stretching, and paced up
and down in front of the cook stove. "I like it, Cliff, I like it a lot. Can
you read it one more time?"

143

And so, I repeated it, only this time I lingered in the story as if it was happening again beside her gurney in the ER. When I was done, there was a prolonged silence in the room. He sat listening as the fire sputtered and cracked alive but was beginning to die down to coals in the open fireplace.

"You really did it," he said, out of the blue. "I saw the girl, I really saw the girl." With enthusiasm his face lighted up with pure expression of being honest. "Pretty good," he added, looking through a stack of paper the middle of the table near the saltshaker. "One good poem deserves another," he said, pulling one out, and he broke into the poem.

"Tell me," she said, "tell me now."
With her hands clenched childlike
Ready for anything wanting the truth
The silence went deep like a blade
That it wasn't there I couldn't say
The words in my mind were gone
That my mouth could not create
She waited her body stiff as stone
Already knowing but needing to hear
She sat down near the fireplace
With the flames that danced orange
And something went out of her then
Like she'd turned into a little girl
This child that won't no matter what
That thing about knowing that isn't
When it's all about touching holding
This truth that doesn't need the words
That children know before they grow
That I saw that child come back in her
As she sat in the chair leaning back
And the void just became sparrows

My throat became a sky full of blue
Flying this child wingless in the sounds
That it won't leave this I'm afraid of
Though I want to with all my might
She hears clearly in what I don't say
She who hears what the heart says
Only that she hears clearer in silence.

He stopped and my mind kept on in the images he created to the scene of the woman in the chair changing to a child, working that psychological shift in details that fit. I kept going back since I knew what he was saying and even related it to instances I'd never noticed before. Now, I could fit it in my experience with his sharp insight. He looked at me, waiting for my appraisal.

"Heavy poem," I said, playing it safe since I was over my head.

"Heavy feeling-wise or heavy with meaning?" he probed.

"Both," I said, and I wasn't sure if that was all. "There's too much for me to digest in a short time. Golly, I'm still stuck there where she turns into a child, ah," I continued, but I was running out of words.

"You don't have to make excuses," he said, cutting me off. "Honesty between poets is essential, let me try one more. See what you think about this one, it's simpler."

Velvet in the sky full of sighs
Twinkle wishing each one's gift
Part light part black between
This sky now all that is and isn't
I can't and I don't know why
The clues in Orion and Polaris
Tell but secrets are for keeping

Your eyes in the back retina caught
Which more you know only so well
All those whys each one at a time
Even when sleep becomes you still
You're so much of the silk past midnight
Unafraid of the beast or the lightning
Promises which night lips speak many
Words like shooting stars make magic
Then it goes back and the still resides
Full circles always beginning or ending
How I feel like dying in the night bright
And then you smile and I forget it all.

"Wow," I couldn't help but saying when he was done. "Wow, you kept it going and it hung together, nice."

He leaned back, smiled, and put it on the stack of papers. Then, it was time for me to get going.

"Dave," I said, "thanks for sharing those poems, wow. I liked that last one, but I gotta get going, the images are calling." I started stretching, slid my bag around my belt ,and pushed to the back so my arms would be free to swing.

Dave looked up, kinda surprised at my sudden exclamation. His face showed that he would have liked to have me around. But the pull was there and I couldn't help myself when I felt it. I shook his hand, saying, "Thanks for inviting me, for the cocoa, reading your poems, and for listening to mine. It was fun."

"Yeah, thanks, I had a good time. See you Thursday night. See ya, Cliff," he added, following me to the door.

As I picked my way over the partially melting road, I thought how poetry allows one to view a person, as he had let me view him. That aloof person that showed up on Thursdays was not him either any more than it was me. I jumped over a large puddle, reached the main road, and continued going on the wet road over the next rise to where there was a ridge that I climbed.

CHAPTER 20

Home for Christmas – A False Start

Dad mailed me a bus ticket for a one-way trip to Florida, and the day was now fast approaching to leave on that trip. Tomorrow crept up on me like a fox. I made the rounds of all my friends to say goodbye and get a hug. Jan had left with her dad to go to LA, and left a note on her door.

There was a foreboding in my mind about the trip to see Mom and Dad, as there would be no place for me to hide. Worse, I didn't know anything about where they had moved, like I would have in Paonia with old girlfriends and places I knew to go to with all their memories. No, it didn't feel good from the start. It would be the same old thing as before with them prying into what was my plan was and why I wasn't achieving more.

When Buffy came with his cousin to see me off, I wasn't happy—not that they came, since that meant a lot to me as they sat there with their noncommittal faces expressionless, as the bus rumbled and spumed exhaust fumes. I should have seen how that in itself was a big deal—two Mescalero Apaches seeing off this white guy, but I was too constricted with my own future dilemma that was coming at me to see the beauty.

I waited for Buffy to say goodbye as I got in line, ready to board, and he walked over as the line got shorter and shorter. Just before I got on, I glanced over and we gave each other a nod but no goodbye. I got on and found a seat toward the back and settled in as the bus shifted through the gears and began rock into motion. It worked its way through the narrow streets barely missing people, and as I got near the outskirts of Santa Fe, then it bothered me that it had been me that hadn't said goodbye, and suddenly I walked down the aisle to the bus driver.

"I left something important back in town," I said earnestly to him.

"Ah," he answered, looking up into the rear view and slowing down.

"Could I get my ticket back, so I can catch the next bus?" I added.

He pulled over, gave me the ticket, and opened the door to the cold. I got out and headed back, feeling easier, almost relieved retracing my path on Pecos Road. I wandered back under the streetlights to the Indian pad on Patio Street. Buffy had his arm around his girlfriend from the Santa Clara Pueblo, sitting there on a couch as the gas heater threw out an orange light. He looked up at me, surprised and smiled and walked over to me.

I gave him a hug, "I didn't say goodbye, so I came back to say it." I turned and headed for the door, stopped, "See you when I get back." I opened the door and crossed the gravel driveway, then I toward my old pad, going by where Norm lived, just in case he was home since it was on the way. I took the driveway in front of his apartment and knocked on the door. I could hear music coming out as a person wailed on a saxophone, hinging runs and rhythms that built and then let go to build again.

Norm opened the door and looked out into the night, "Oh, it's you," he said. "Come on in. Weren't you on your way to Florida?" I walked in and felt the warmth of the little apartment. "Yes, I was," I said, as a girl came out of the kitchen eating a sandwich.

"This is Jenny Cassavas," he said, motioning to her as she came over and tucked her arm under and around Norm's and nodded a greeting.

"I'm Cliff Alexander, glad to meet you," I said, looking into her eyes.

"Jenny happens to be my lady of the hour," Norm added, giving her a hug. They both had a good laugh, like it was a private joke between them. "Want a hit?" he said, holding up a marijuana joint that he had rolled. "Mind you, we use this for medicinal purposes."

Jenny took it out of his hand and put it to her mouth and sucked in. The smoke rolled out the end of the joint between her tight red lips. She offered it to me, and I gave it a drag as she had. Then I gave it to Norm, as the music took on a richer and deeper tone with the notes that stood more alone. I leaned back and let the music work, my mind going with the flow of notes.

Norm had a good conversation going with Jenny so I quietly observed the Monet painting on the wall, and the book of poems on the table in front of me and the grey linoleum floor that was opposite the gas heater with the flicker of an orange flame you could see in the amber glass. Many a night I'd curled up in front of it, lying sideways cozy and snug with one hand between my knee and the other under my head cradling it.

I perused Jenny's features as they bantered back and forth, engaged in an argument about classical or commercial music and how with the commercial there is always a hook in the chorus and how classical the music is pure and existed solely because it belongs.

Jenny would be hard to describe since there was nothing special about her. If I were to describe her, that's my description. Plain Jenny would be a good pseudonym except she compensated for her generic looks by the way she expressed herself—she was animated, and she was a comedian with a natural sense of timing to her come-backs. Her punch lines would come at will in spontaneous response to Norm, who would pan his face in a natural expression as if he hadn't got it, only to come back with a comment that would get her going, only to pull back with a blank look on his face, as if she was ranting alone about nothing.

It wasn't long before I was truly caught up in their verbal sparring match that they had going on, as they each in their special way, were on a roll. I became an audience of one and started laughing as they one-upped each other only to get another shot. It was the kind of humor riveted in the moment, that you had to be there to get the general tone, and the back-and-forth of a faked insult or innuendo. Norm would mockingly insult Jenny, who would not let on one bit that Norm had gotten to her, only to ask him a question about his expertise in a subject area and then wait as he tried to convince her of his acumen. The scene died down as Jenny had to go to the bathroom to freshen up.

"Hey," Norm said, "How come you're not on the bus headed to Florida?"

"I got on, but I got nervous and had to back off, to say goodbye to Buffy," I answered in a stuttering, roundabout way that made no sense.

"Going home is not an easy thing to do," Norm said, taking another hit. Jenny came out as he was finishing. "I haven't been back," he hesitated and got a sad look on his face. Jenny put her arm around him to hug him, looking at his expression. "Dad was a union man that worked the steel in high-rise buildings," he went on, "and you could say that I would never measure up to him, so," he sighed deeply, "see what I mean, it just isn't easy going back."

I nodded, seeing what he was trying to get over to me and he was right.

"I couldn't hold a candle to what he was able to accomplish. He couldn't write a poem if his life depended on it, nor did he want to, and that's why I never had a problem with being on my own in the world. Since I wasn't accepted a home, I had to find my acceptance elsewhere. Poetry was good, since it was an emotional outlet for my frustration, as well as it gave me an avenue from which I found people like me whose love of poetry is imprinted permanently in their makeup. You might say that same bond is what you and I have. Really, what do I know about you, except that you love poetry? Last time I went home, old age had weakened Dad's mind and body. He ended up a beat man, as he couldn't maintain his high standards. So, you see, I know full well why you had to get off that bus and drop by,"

"But," I interrupted, but he interrupted my interrupting by adding, "I know you're going to go. You'll have to, you just have to do it like that salmon swimming back from the middle of the Pacific Ocean to some no name creek in the middle of Alaska to spawn and then die." He took another hit then added, "We're pretty funny that way; we act like big shots, when in some ways, we make as much sense as that salmon alone up a creek in the middle of nowhere."

He took another hit off the bottom end of the joint and sucked in hard, as the musician on the record went on an intricate run on the sax. All three of us found the music a joining experience, as we sat transfixed the way music can be when its rhythm mystics its notes into your psyches. It was a Zen-like experience in my mind, as I contemplated Norm's words that kept going over and over in my mind. In the end, it wasn't about Buffy except on a superficial level and the fact that his friendship as a Mescalero Apache meant a lot to me. Dad had always spoke of the Mescalero with pride in his voice. How they were a proud and a fiercely loyal group with discipline. Being a friend with me being white told me something about myself —that there was something in me of worth that I too could believe in.

I couldn't help but see Norm's deeper truth at work too, as I sat there. Then like that, I felt like going and getting some sleep for tomorrow, so that I would be ready for that trip back, as now my mind was right. I knew what it was about, and I could see myself clearer this time.

"Thanks, Norm," I said, getting up and buttoning up my coat, getting ready for the cold outside, as Norm looked over from his conversation with Jen.

At the door I turned and walked over and gave him a hug and shook Jenny's hand, this time with feeling, not holding back as before due to my safe judgmental mental gymnastics to keep another person at bay. Out into the clear night and the blinking stars under the streetlights and barking dogs, I walked back to my garage apartment by myself with my dreams just as fragile. Later in that night I dreamed good, and didn't fear the void that could enter.

The Second Try

I sat there towards the back of the bus, listening to the roll of the diesel pistons and watching the exhaust spume in a cloud outside into the cold until we got moving through the narrow streets on to the highway.

Then it started, as the miles narrowed in my mind like that salmon. The bus took over, with the miles sliding under the tires rolling fast. Shifting up the gears, foot on the pedal, blinking behind his Ray Bans, the driver kept the momentum constant as the fields, towns all went by. As gas stations, fences, livestock wandering between wide horizons all flew by my vantage point, I saw the contours of the land rhymed with

153

the vegetation. Mesquites were in groves and yucca out in the drier spots, cactus spine or cat claw differing in a shade of green and structure all gathered and disappeared as we went by.

As the greens got deeper and the leaves fuller while we continued east, the land gave way to lush grasses, fat sleek cows, hardwood forests that crowded the edge of the road, so that I couldn't see far, and I felt the humidity climb as I got out at a rest stop and bought a soda. There was a layover in New Orleans, and I got out of the station in front and looked at the city lights and the chaos of the range of people who, in the midst of this randomness, seemed to know what they were about. Right away I was over my head so I went back into the station and sat down. In the lobby I sat alone and let the red sweeping minute hand captivate me. As the minutes passed, I felt the pit of my stomach get even tighter until 2:00 a.m. hit and it was time to get back on the bus and find a seat.

Back Home?

Dad was waiting for me at the bus station in his patient, quiet, unassuming way. I felt his true concern and the pressure it put on me scared me bad—(I just couldn't hide the scars of getting beat up in max). There was no turning back from what happened in that stockade and the demons that I knew not how to deal with—only that I had a loathing for myself now, and how was I going to tell Dad about that. This person I now was, was like this raw nerve unable to fake it, much unlike that fun-loving, carefree son they had once known.

We drove to their new home in silence as I had nothing to relate to here. In Paonia, there would have been talk of the cows, the hay yield, the thrills of looking back on the feats of my youth and the memories that they held for me. Here, this was a place for the memories of my father, for it was here that he first met my mom when he was in aviator school at Pensacola and she was a nurse at the hospital. Inside, I went

154

headlong into what expectations that would now never be, taking a deep breath.

I walked down the hallway full of his plaques of this and that, many of which were his Navy awards, full of all the past that now could hold what his life had been, but not me. I went up to Mom, rushed the moment, giving her a hug so that she would not take in more than I was able to fake.

In the disjointed conversations as I gazed out a window, Mom found out, in the void of enthusiasm, something had changed. I couldn't help that I just didn't care about the same things, even as our conversations ended up trailing off to nowhere. I spaced out, wandering to thoughts about my life back in Santa Fe.

I found combing beaches for the remnants of a last squall helped, with me among the waves, finding shells in wadded seaweed gobs. All the while the seagulls *ka, ka*ed, as they took off into the wind flying with the forces, always their eyes on what was edible below, not ever missing the smallest crab or what was left over of a picnic. Time went easy, even easier than it had in Santa Fe.

But still, as a farm boy from Colorado, I felt out of place hanging out there after a while, and that bored dull emptiness invaded my gut. When I got home, Mom and Dad had come to a consensus that I could tell it was over except, that I had been invited for Christmas. Somehow we all knew, though nothing was ever said and even intimated. It was that feeling of resigned realization on their part.

One night me and Laurie, my younger sister, played Santana on the stereo, and we turned the 33 and a third to sixteen speed and spaced the notes so that you could really get into the movements of Santana's song *Samba Pa Ti*. As we lay on the carpet beside the stereo, our hands touched in the darkness. She also found out that her older brother was now a weakened sparrow with the pressure her hands telling me, with the strength of the music that somewhere in this. That was all that could be said without any talking between a brother and his little sister.

Back to the Deep Water

When Dad drove me to the depot, we were both relieved the time had come. There was a distinct acceptance from him that both scared and helped me as we hugged. I felt that scratchy stubble from his cheek against mine as the tune of the diesel engines idling in the background spumed exhaust.

I waved to him as the bus took off—him standing quietly there, waving back, watching his son going back out into deep water, conflicted with so much at once, armed with the twenty that he gave me to get something on the way back. It was off into the miles of USA that ribbons of asphalt held, wheels spinning the way the Greyhound's did; covering miles rolling to destinations. As Santa Fe got closer with each mile, that thrill grew inside along with that fear that the darkness could still descend and leave nothing left.

I noticed my hand begin to shake as I looked out at the running contours that ran with erosion or wind-drifted sand. Insight spoke of rejuvenation or of renewed determination whose images I fed on so that the shaking subsided. I was reminded by the closeness of that edge of giving up, how important the secrets I saw out the window were to me that Dad would never have understood. To him, this unseen weakness of mine was just senseless, except that it was horribly real. It made my eye, out the window, catch the least and weave it to meaning.

My sensitivity tuned now in the moment to find where the links would fit which cruxes turned upon themselves and sourced out, making sense to me. That was the marrow that burned in my blood and was my only hope for now. And so, the wheels spun to the tune of the diesel pistons that powered on gears—shifting past Dallas, Abilene, Clovis, Clines Corners, then Moriarty and towards Albuquerque, where I'd switch buses for one heading north to Santa Fe.

As the bus went by the Santo Domingo turn-off, I could feel the whirl tell me that the battle was coming and that it was for real. I took a deep breath and held it; none other would do nor could I rest even for a second in hesitation. The downer could start at any time and pull me hard like quicksand so the bars that were invisible in way were still a part of me. As the contours went by, the mesquite, roving washes, sagebrush soft grey or raven flight gathered together outside the window breathed with their own stories that I found real and captivating. They held me captive to a world that gave me hope, gave me renewal, along with my Mescalero Apache friend behind his indefinite quiet blank look that no one could penetrate unless he allowed you in on his own.

That it all spoke of an ungiving-up within me that kept my gyro spinning. As the Greyhound wheels spun to the diesel rumble going up gears shifting to keep the momentum gaining on the sharp incline north, I felt life coming back to me. Words were there waiting to free me with that fear split second holding one versus the vacant selling-out this battle ever alive, why Santa Fe was so important ten miles away.

CHAPTER 21

Santa Fe in my Blood

As I got off the bus, the cold that hit me and took my breath away. There was no doubt since I left that the winter had taken a turn for the worse, as the crusty snow was everywhere and icicles were dangling from all the gutters. On every eave, crystal droplets dripped down where they spattered like diamonds in the last crack of light from the afternoon that was sliding into evening.

I headed back to my apartment behind the crazy ladies in the adobe house, pretty much accepted that this salmon had not found his spawning ground.

Reclining on the bed, looking outside for the familiar view, I let the spin of the events that kept coming at me to slow down. Looking back, there was something that didn't happen that I thought would. Never mind, I had found the old me just didn't work anymore—that was gone like a distant vision of that carefree youth that had once been there. In a way that was what I had been afraid to find, and yet now it didn't bother me at all.

Regain Some Ground

The next day the sun made the ground come alive with reflections, pure white humps here and there, mystically hiding the plants and walls. I put on my wool sweater and the rainbow hat from Goodwill, and out into the frozen waste I braved, taking a deep breath. Loving every bit, I wandered towards town on a semi-plowed street over car tracks, as the wind blew skiffs of snow from roofs out into open expanse.

My hands were deep into my pockets and my shoulders hunched. My feet crunched over the dry remnants of last night's flurries. Getting closer to town, the traffic picked up, as cars made their way. The drivers held their hands tight on the steering wheels ready for and sudden slide that might occur.

I made my rounds from the library magazines, Walgreens, to La Fonda and came up cold, finding no one with which to catch up on events, so I gave up and started catching up on shops I hadn't been to in a while.

Going up stairs, opening the door with the little bell on the upper part, I went into a sandalwood-smelling atmosphere of the Asian import shop off Ortiz where I could stand in front of a Tibetan Mandala. I watched images as they, in their contrasting colors, pulled my attention and worked magic on the periphery. The outer images seemed to move and the inner ones changed expression with their fiery beards and swinging swords with eyes that stared at me. I barely found the Buddha sitting peacefully in the middle, smiling, centered to the spot in the middle of my forehead. If I held my line, the piece moved on its own. The clerk shifted position and the seat squeaked while she read from her book about herbal remedies.

I was close to that fine line between losing myself and finding middle ground but I gave up on my discovery of self via the mandala since I was short on discipline that it takes. I glanced at the clerk who still concentrated on her book and quietly left.

Outside, I noticed that time had flown and it was now midmorning and a wave of heat was causing the transitions to go full force. I caught sight of large drops from melting icicles, cascading where they spattered and flew apart, splashing, thrashing down below through the grate of the drains in the gutter.

The air was full of the sound of melting as large droplets from the icicles fell where they gathered in the gutter, making a swishing noise. My wet feet ran numb cold up through my legs, looking everywhere and seeing the reasons I kept moving. I rode this spark in my conscious, my retina finding a myriad of forms—the swooshing of cars, coursing the rivulets, splashing crystals, capturing prisms in the gutters, as shoppers went on their ways.

For me, I was in another world in a different time frame, creatively riding the insights from this river whose current was carrying me on.

Right Place Right Time

I turned west, going east on Alameda til I got to the Old Santa Fe Trail Street. Then I headed north til I came to Shelby Street and kept going. The clouds were beginning to pick up and thicken with dark bellies. On past the La Fonda Hotel, I went, knowing I was short on money, and I crossed the street. I continued across Palace Avenue where Washington intersected it. On the left was the library and across the street a street café that had the best lentil soup that, on a day like today, stuck to your ribs. I opened the door to the tune of bells that hung on a thick wire and found a booth in the corner where I still had a view of the street with the people coming and going in the mid-part of this busy day, You could tell in the rhythm of the people the holidays had exacted a toll as Santa Fe peeled back its mortal side under the impersonations and theoretical conversations alleging intelligence that went nowhere, that only served to create a façade that an intellectual was lurking within.

When Jan came out to take my order, I was really surprised to see her. She wore a man's white dress shirt with a set of suspenders and her hair up. A pencil was balanced on the upper part of her ear with a smile on her face.

"Hi, when did you get on?" I asked, seeing how the shirt fit nicely on her.

"Right after semester break, I figured I could use the money, so here I am. What'a you gonna have?" she said leaning over putting the pad on the table.

"I want a bowl of that lentil soup, with plenty of crackers," I added, looking up at her. As I waited, I let my eyes wander outside. The flakes

161

were flying and the people going by had a more hunched-over posture to their gait.

She came back and put the soup in front of me, adding, "How'd your visit go?"

"Everything's changed. Well, they're the same but I changed. It's hard when it's just not there anymore. It didn't help that they moved to Florida and I don't know anything about the area," I said.

"Yeah, tell me about it. I went back for a weekend, and you're right. Some things changed, and some were just the same like they were holding on and afraid to see what might come," she said, looking over at another customer. "I'll be back," she said, "Enjoy your soup."

The soup was a real treat, and I ate it with plenty of crushed-up crackers on top. Eating the soup and watching the snow come down outside was better than TV.

The Plot Thickens

Two guys and a girl came in, all wearing dark glasses, brushing off the snow from their shoulders. The girl looked like David's chick, and they sat down right behind me in the next booth without noticing me. Both guys she was with had on a dark suits and sported Ray Ban glasses. I glanced at her hand and sure enough there was that heart tattoo with the arrow through it. They were talking as they came in and continued as they settled in the booth.

"Don't worry," she said, shifting her voice to a quieter level, barely audible, "Everything's under control, and is going on as planned. Like I said before, I have him eating out of my hand like a puppy. When I pull the carpet out, he's going fall a long way." She dropped her voice as Jan approached.

A man's voice took over, as Jan took their order, "We'll have coffee, one with sugar and make mine black, and one with cream and

162

sugar." As Jan left, the man added, "How can you be so sure?" He said emphasizing sure.

"You don't know the meaning of the word infiltration, until you see me at work. Now that I've got this guy in love with me, along with that stuff you're giving me, when I pull out, there'll be nothing left." She added, "I do find a problem that's beginning to develop I hadn't counted on."

"What's that?" he asked lowing his voice, as Jan slid the coffee cups on the counter.

"This guy is different than the others. The others were cold and already hardened. David has a softness to him that's real. I'm not so sure I can pull this off."

"But you said there would be nothing left when you got through with him."

"That's just it. You don't understand. To you he's just a job that needs completing," she said taking a deep breath. "There's a vulnerability to him I hadn't counted on."

"I'm not sure I like what I'm hearing. You know that we pay you good money."

"I know that," she said. "I can't help it. I'm falling for him, and I can't help it."

"Look," he said firmly. "What this kid knows could put a lot of people behind bars. A lot of important people that he doesn't even know could go and do hard time. If it got out, dominoes would fall all over the place. He knows just too much."

She laughed, "Funny thing is that he doesn't know that he knows."

"The people I work for see no humor in going to jail, and he could put them there. Anyway, you're not getting paid to think, you're getting paid to. . .," he hesitated.

She cut in, "To be affectionately available for him, and that's what I'm good at." She added defiantly, "But it's still going to be hard for me, and I can't help it. Why can't you just go with plan A?"

"Because we can't arise any suspicions," he persisted. "It's got to look like it was all his doing." He stopped short and waited for her response.

"Okay, okay, I'll still go through with it as planned," she admitted, sipping coffee.

"Remember slip small doses at first so that he slowly feels it slide sideways," the man said, sliding something over toward her in a brown envelope.

I started getting an empty feeling in my stomach seeing that David was in her sights. If she saw me, things could get real complicated, so I finished the soup. When she excused herself to go to the lady's room, I made my break, going to the register and slid the check to Jan.

"Forget it," she said. "Just don't be late tonight when you come by tomorrow, okay?"

"Seven o'clock sharp," I said, looking into her deep brown eyes looking back. I felt like leaning over to give her a kiss, as she leaned back and put her finger to her lips smiling, shaking her head no, giving me a wink before I turned to go.

CHAPTER 22

Over to David's

I was back on partially melting streets, as the sun had come out full again and the infrared was causing steam to rise off the dark asphalt into the air. Cars went through steam with the sounds of splashing slush and dripping gutters. I headed towards Canyon Road with this new development to ponder.

My breath clouded up and my shoes made crunching sounds on the sidewalk that had about six good inches of dry powder. As I went further from town, the cold ceased to be a factor as the exertion built up my internal energy. With the exception of my cold feet from my wet shoes, I was doing okay.

Except now, I was faced with the task of telling David that his girlfriend sucked and that she was talking about dumping him when he was most vulnerable. *Crap*, I thought, going by adobe houses with chimneys curling smoke and barking dogs that gave a perfunctory bark from their warm spot. I had to smile as I considered that even animals have their lines drawn.

Up the long slope I went and could see his place in front of a high mesa that rose like a large cat ready to pounce on its prey. The paranoia was getting into my head. As I got closer, I pondered how I'd never let myself be so vulnerable. I was a penny-ante, one-dimensional, get-through-the-moment-in-one-piece guy, but I knew what I had to do as I got closer to his place going past his wood pile. I knocked on the door and waited, hearing rustling sounds inside.

The door opened and he looked out, not surprised at my presence, which surprised me, "How's it going?" I asked innocently.

"I kind'a figured you'd come by," he said, "How'd the trip back home go? Come in, I got the fire burning nice and hot."

I sat down at his table and he got the tea pot and poured it in a cup, and put in a tea bag. Steam billowed steam over the cup's brim.

"Thanks," I said. "It went okay, but things had changed for me so it wasn't."

"I know what you're saying. But you gotta know, it hadn't changed at all. The changes are inside of you. Home stays the same, it doesn't change. I got to hand it to you, though, you've got guts; that's for sure," he took a sip from his cup and looked back, waiting for a response.

Funny, when someone knows your plight, there's no need for explaining. I smiled and took a sip from the tea and let the flavors take their places.

"Growing up's a bitch," I came up with. "It wasn't there like it used to be."

"Guess what? Neither is anything else." He added, looking at a cigar box. It seemed to be full of photos as I glanced at it closer. "That's why I figured you came by. Was just a matter of time," he added, "before you put it together. Only another poet would have caught the clue from why I used that color orange, when it didn't make any sense at all."

166

"But," I stammered, trying to break in the flow of his thoughts for a gap.

"You know," he went on, "We're a lot alike, both of us are naïve as hell. I sensed that right off, even with your—I-don't-give-a-crap attitude." I looked over at the fire as it was dying down, cracking less intense. "If I hadn't loved being out there in the first place, it wouldn't've…," he trailed off, gazed at the fire, and put another log on it.

By now, I figured he had something that he had wanted to tell me, so I sat there, sipping tea waiting to see where it was going to go, since he was right. We were much alike, he could even be a lost brother.

He came back and picked up one of the pictures. I could see the face of a Vietnamese man dressed in an officer's uniform with ribbons on his pocket.

"The color you picked up on," he went on, "was the safe one for me since the real one, red, was just way too real, too starkly true." He poured tea in his cup and a splash of Jack Daniels. "Here," he said, "it'll smooth it out."

I took the Jack Daniels and poured some into mine and I took a sip. I could feel it burn way down in my throat, generating warmth inside. Before I knew it, a collage of snapshots from the stockade were coming.

As he showed me pictures of Vietnamese soldiers, he didn't know it, but my wounds were opening that I thought I had healed, that I had left at that on ramp in Raton in August. I felt an urge to get up and run, but I could tell David was in trouble, like that a rookie swimmer in the midst of a rip tide losing the battle. I was over my head, but in a way, I had no choice in the matter.

He took a measured breath after taking another sip, and tightened his lips. "How'd I know that I would get good at killing people? It just happened. It got me out there, where I'd be by myself and fit into the environment. Lining up the cross hairs, just like before with a deer in the sights," he said, holding up his arms as if he had a rifle there, aiming, pulling a trigger.

He looked up. "A picture, coordinates, and an x on a contour map was all that they gave me, but then I knew that I was free and I'd be left alone." I was just beginning to see what he was trying to get at, as he went on. "I heard there was a sixty-thousand-dollar bounty on my head, dead or alive. It's red—the color that I was afraid to use that you saw right through."

He had been right. It was the poet thing that made me go right there. "That war screwed us up," I said, thinking of that guard that beat me. I could tell he was waiting for me to say something, but it wouldn't come.

He put his head in his hands and the silence grew, as the fire burned. "There's not a day that I don't see one of their faces looking right at me with that expression they had before I pulled the trigger and ended it. Sometimes they all come a once, and I don't know what to do about it."

Then we both sat a while looking at the fire as flames cracked and sputtered, finding the places the sap would explode its life force, sending a shooting red ember in front of us that hissed, as a tail of grey smoke curled up, then went completely out.

He leaned back absorbed, as the fire found the secret places of the tree that sang out its days of changing climate, its roots translated into rings what kind of summer it had been now uncoiled traces up the chimney.

"You know," he broke the silence, sighing, "I never thought of this but. . ." He stopped, going back into his thoughts as the flames danced in front.

I was thinking about myself in the stockade, going to that dark place. It seemed the fire allowed me to push that moment closer than before to that place where I'd be undone, where there'd be nothing left of me, where I went to zero. I saw myself there, as the flames ran orange to purple and climbed out.

Dave said something, but I couldn't make it out, as if I was a long way off. For that moment, I was there, and I started to cry at that scared guy I saw. I heard Dave crying too, but I was too far away, in that place a long time ago. I did not ask why, as I took one last look way back there as he went about how to survive, seeing myself in the mixing light and the heat in past tense—that kid who hadn't measured up to what he knew to be true, falling short.

I found suddenly that I couldn't hate him like I had done without any pity. My crying was like the fire as it searched that moment it went wrong. It hit me that it didn't even matter anymore as I gathered myself, and then it occurred to me that David had been crying too in long subdued sobs. He looked over at me and composed himself. "Somethings you just can't take back, huh?" he half-whispered.

"David," I said interrupting, "I gotta go now." And I stretched and walked over where he was sitting with tears rolling down his face. I offered him my hand. We hugged for a while as if we were holding something much greater than either of us knew and that, if we let go, it might all disappear and we'd be like before. Then we let go, and I walked out into the dark night.

I walked in the light of a half-moon where I could see enough ahead so I could avoid the still thawed puddles from the day's warmth.

As I came down and around a bend, Santa Fe opened up with its lights. Santa Fe was all huddled up with smoke spewing out of its chimneys on this clear January night, this town that went back to the trading posts and the Catholic priests building chapels with their visions of conversion left from Cortez's attempt to find the gold that he knew was near. I walked midst the Spanish-influenced architecture in the adobe houses, and I kept going where the houses got closer and the neighborhoods more clustered.

A Gypsy Detour

I took a short-cut turn up a street off of Alameda, mulling my thoughts. Going back to what I had allowed myself to relive helped me feel stronger now. I went past a cantina and heard guitar music that sounded Castilian, as I caught strains of emotion from a man who sang along to it with his deep guttural riffs that wove into the music and drew me inside.

The candlelight lit the scene barely visible. I wandered to the bar in front of mirror walls that had a glass shelf with all sorts of whiskey bottles displayed. People were clapping as the man was pounding on his guitar. Intent on keeping the beat, the man kept as he sang along too.

The bartender came over giving me eye contact, "A *cerveza*," I said. He came back with a glass with golden liquid in the soft light that came from the stage where the guy was playing solo. Clicking of heels on the floor in a staccato rhythm came loudly. I squinted into the dark, thinking *this is too much*. As I was trying to focus on the half-lit stage, a girl came into view whose features looked familiar, so that I stared, trying to figure where I'd met her.

Her oval eyes, high cheek bones, erect and well-endowed carriage—I couldn't pull my stare off, as she danced with increasing intensity. The guitar man got into his riffs as if he was going crazy. He kept singing deeply. Then it hit me, the girl that I met in the library. *Ah, Gabrielle.*

Along with the clicking of her heels, she spun with cassinettes clicking also. The music built to a crescendo as the people clapped with the riveting beat that kept on building with the intensity of movement, almost hypnotically. Then like that, it stopped and the audience erupted in applause standing and some saying "*Bueno, Bueno.*"

Such electricity, I couldn't believe, as I was totally enthralled by her aplomb. Gabrielle bowed and then disappeared behind flowing, black curtains. The man played on, but I was in awe of what I had witnessed, wanting more, but my eyes got tired in the half-lit room. I wandered outside back to my route home under the streetlights, heading southwest. As I walked on, how Gabrielle danced had me thinking of her in a whirl of thoughts and snapshots. Had I not recognized her, I wouldn't have guessed that had been her—how she danced with so much confidence and certainty of movement. In the library I'd seen a softer side. This side scared me, as I was a nobody, a person who could at best catch a glimpse at life and spin it into words.

I was quick silver, she was twenty-carat gold, I figured under the trees that rattled their pods and made scratching sounds that came and went as I came to the open courtyard that led to my garage apartment. I got inside and remembered the conversation I'd overheard in the café earlier, and how I had completely forgotten to tell David.

CHAPTER 23

Falling Down

It was a slow Thursday night, as people trickled inside, reminding me of the ER and the boredom of a slow shift. Hesitantly I looked around at who else was there to sense the electricity level. As usual, you can't tell when dealing with poetry that can turn on a dime so the fair- weathered fans were the superficial ones that really didn't matter.

This was perfect for a poet, since the power of his work will hold uncommitted listeners who will respond only to what really works inside. They will think nothing about getting up right in the middle of a dead poem and walking out the door. Honestly, that's really what it's all about anyhow—cold turkey reading the words and getting that small window of opportunity for the projections to spin meanings up, so the drama can justify inflection and hold like steel. In the end that's what it's all about anyhow.

It was about eight o'clock, and Norm and David were still yet to show up. The winter had taken its toll as weary looks witnessed cold nights and shivered days, getting through the recent storms with its blizzarded skies. Norm came in with a certain zest in his step and gave me a solid welcome.

"Good to see you. How'd the trip back go?" he gave me a smile that he already knew that I couldn't answer him in the limitations of here.

I nodded, giving him a feeling that I had found out important things. In a way, there was a greater sense of freedom than before going back. I had a little more acceptance of reasons that things had to be this way or more, so that this was a situation that I actually preferred, even loved in place where it was happening right now.

He walked over to the podium and tapped on the mike softly. "Good evening, folks. Hope you had a good one and all that," he smiled in his cut-through-the-crap way, that he didn't really care but he was getting the energy going. If that's what it took, then so be it. "Let's see," he said, looking over at me as David with that blonde on his arm came in and sat down to the side in the shadows that flickered in the room. "Yeah," he added, "Cliff will start out the night, so let's hear it for him."

I was surprised, but grabbed my stack of poems and got up there.
Seagram's in the mix comes down warm
Some space allotted me in the changes
Her face my thoughts a little thirsty
That silk could quench my wondering
Out of the blue there you are dancing
Midnight in your eyes moving sinewy
That your rhythm whispers of wishes
Going on and on changing just enough
Balance and leaning sequences next
Ever so dangerously so that I can tell
Your next move intense reading you
Just what it is that lingers in your gaps
That completely free next spontaneous
So the rhyme fits not any holding back
That smile knowing it's there on its way

Mysterious magnets working the forces
How what is meant to be comes anyhow
For the sequence is its own fortune teller
Merging of lines where there were none
Angles and smiles recognizing the signs
This minuet where everything's to lose
Taking that risk just the same, going for it
Slender moment when it's all on the line
You and me and there rolling the dice
Tumbling as the fates work the variables
That piece their way aligning of hearts
Where they never really know but compel
Moths to the light so they are drawn
To this flame within that will never go out
We that dance to this fire we can't see.

The poem ended and I let the words run out like a runner who just finished the race and had nowhere else to push. The images solid with what I was trying to say, vague enough so the options were automatically in place to pivot off them fast, to keep it loose enough so that you couldn't really tell what was coming.

I sat down to scattered applause as some continued conversing. Connections, it's all about establishing connections

Norm gave me a nod, indicating I'd got the ball rolling sufficiently. He ambled to the mike and pulled out a paper. "Here," he said, "I've got one that I'd like to share with you."

Norms

Down the upside of her smiles
Sideways in the choices of expression
Pulling back or holding just in front

Just enough of her lightning the moment
Always juxtaposed replying angling off
Unexpected changing in the very middle
Immediately taking me whole right now
Fire and stirring her arms around me
I shut my eyes and imagine her soul
Mixing with mine in this fleshed caldron
Soaring midst this mere of what I am
Her signs my winged flight beyond safety
No nets below only this dark bottom
Thrilling independent just making out
What might in all the paradoxes at once
Be that fool that I am free and captive
Exempting not myself in what's at stake
Ever just so midflight for all I'm worth.

The applause was tremendous, and he had put his soul out there in the way he had read the words, infusing them with his zest to let all see that vulnerability the listeners were responding to. I saw right then why his poem had pulled everyone to risk it all with him. I had read mine, describing as I went clearly but with no soul. I filed that lesson away silently, realizing that it was good to see that Norm was back riding high in his images—still that bull-in-the-social-grace china shop, blasting away nonstop, unafraid to mispronounce or to run in a new way to communicate with a lookout-below, ready-or- not, here-I-come attitude. As much as his words was the fact that he put himself out there, vulnerable as he could be, in his celebration of language's power while he still painted the picture in the language.

He nodded, acknowledging the audience, aware of chemistry as the reason why we were enjoying the play in the words beyond where

175

the breakers broke for a chance to see the images bind with the emotions that fueled between those delicate lines.

I glanced over at Dave with his blonde with her arm entangled in his. By the way his shoulders were hunched, I could tell he had a poem that he was needing to read to see if he could breathe it life with his voice past that scary part of the compulsion to where you're naked out there, stripped to the bone of the merest thought upon which the poem's life rests.

I took a deep breath for him, as he ambled those long steps. Getting there, he tapped the mike to assess the sensitivity level, relaxed, looked down at the podium where he had placed his sheets of paper. Pulling out one, he got a satisfied look like this was the one of all the rest that would sail his heart in this night and ride out through the images. He looked around and said, "Hello, I'm David and happy to be here." Then without saying anything more he looked down and started.

> The air is too thin up here
> Fast up coming to a blur
> "Slow down," the voices say
> Count backward ten nine
> No don't hold your breath
> Don't move and break the spell
> This door Seagram's opens darkly
> Fire across the endings deepens
> Just so I can find my bearings
> This running from person I know
> Shadows coming toward me faster
>
> A sudden center stopping points
> Meditation circling with the ravens
> Fear revolving over this still form

Beyond intentions child of yesterday
Growing ever small in all the nexts
Crying long gone in the never mores
Remade every time our lips meet
What I leave behind you replace
Hold me for now just hold me tight.

When he stopped, we were all breathless, held by his diction that made the words pierce and hold as the images connected and left. When he was through, a glow stayed on with us so that afterward, conversations went less, as the meanings lingered. There was no applause, which was even a greater compliment. David had left a piece of himself up there, exposed and open, which courage goes along the same lines as those facing death, which part scared me for his sake. He nodded and walked over to where his blonde was sitting. He sat down and kissed her, much like a matador does to his significant other after facing down death.

The successive poems after mine made me feel kinda small since they were full of risk, allowing it to be all on the line. I was again safely ensconced behind the images almost invisible. I stopped as I went by David's table.

"Really good job tonight," I said, holding out my hand toward him. I could feel him hold a little longer with his hand than before, like a trapeze artist after defying death—needs to be held too. I noticed that split second not wanting to let go before I turned, but I didn't let on the way guys do when a truth's been revealed.

"Cliff," he said, breaking my attempt to leave, so I stopped, turned. "Wow," he said, "how'd you come up with that sequence is its own fortune teller. Wow, just like a diamond in the rough." He emphasized the point, looking at me.

"Thanks," I said, "I loved your poem. It was too much, David." I slowed my walk out, allowing myself to look around, and caught glances from people as they held their look that told me that on that night I had really made a difference.

Back out into the night where the stars lit a path to my garage home, I walked, this shadowed stranger, on past the dogs toward his home. This night like so many of the others, except there was this magic that made the walk home full of metaphors and whirling paradoxes that all at once collided with a realization that both held and let go independently there in their truth. For that moment was me alive in this first time sight gives birth to what were once secrets that now to me spoke this language that had its own life diction. As I walked on, they became like keys that were unlocking, so that once inside the garage, I went into a wondrous slumber.

CHAPTER 24

Time in the Dish Room

The dish room no longer offered a challenge as it had before. The spoon, forks, knives, each separated beneath the hot suds as my fingers found food that stuck, flicking it off absentmindedly. The radio boomed, *My sweet lord*, the background keeping the beat to the lyrics, *I really want to know you*, (louder) *I really want to see you, Lord*. Between the recognitions of my own conscious thought patterns around the parts of David's poem last night, I remembered especially how he had said the words with his magic voice. Scraping dried-egg residue off the plate, watching it float away, my thoughts slid back to Jan's contours and her soft caring way. Maybe this image I was searching for was closer than I had thought.

I still remembered how she had looked in that tight shirt in the café and how her hint of a smile seemed to tell me more that something new had entered her mind about me that was deeper. So I lingered scouring the thick pot with the abrasive steel wool. Time passed with the clatter of porcelain and the swirl of the suds. I got through the midmorning rush. Now the lunch group was coming and my legs were damp wet and my back was tired from leaning over.

If not for you, the winter would, speakers rattled by, jangling bones, the ups and downs of the dish room framed time, by getting it done til that magic number on the clock ran to three, and I was done. Punching out and checking in the mirror for any last adjustments, fixing my hair and splashing water on my face, and drying off was my usual ritual. I went out to the sidewalks, going by pawn shops and motels north on Cerrillos Road to the burger stand that bordered the Institute of American Indian Arts with its students and their thick black hair and innocent eyes looking deep into mine, holding and springing with a smile and a hello that I mirrored.

Ordering a Dr Pepper and putting that quarter into the juke box, Junior Walker came on, *Going to play it for you*, on his impressive sax, I allowed the day to catch up with my mind. I pulled out my notebook and my faithful BIC pen that never let me down, and the words began in the background. I knew my date with Jan was formulating as I sat thinking of her sultry eyes and her hair that smelled of Chanel Number 9, allowing the mental projections of all the possibilities that could take their way. There was something about her liking me that made the rest a verging reality, worth thinking about.

Turning Points

When seven o'clock arrived—the white knight smelling of Aqua Velva, glancing at the door window with my reflection of my strong cheekbones and broken front tooth. I knocked and thought of my best opening line, in case nothing came, which had often happened in the past. I've now learned for be ready for "Murphy" to interject himself, just in case.

The door opened and Jan appeared in a dark dress with a red scarf. That gave it a touch of class, as well as a note of social indifference. I smiled and looked at her closer and noticed the tint to her cheeks and the high light blue of her eyes and the contours of her breasts, all in one sweeping take-it-in glance.

Her eyes looked past me, allowing me to take in her figure freely, and our eyes met pupil to pupil, and her slight smile widened. As she leaned forward and opened the door, I brushed in past her, feeling her firmness give to my sliding pressure going by.

"Come in," she half whispered. "Go ahead, put on some music. Albums are over there."

As I went through her albums, the smell of meat and potatoes hit me. My expectations climbed as I approached the stereo and browsed. The Houdini part of me was plotting a way out of any traps that were getting laid—you know that testosterone-radar thing. I put on Aretha Franklin on and grabbed a magazine to peruse.

"Beef tongue is my best dish," she said, adding, "Do you know why?"

"Ah," I said, not really knowing, looking up from glossy pictures.

"It's the cost," she said proudly. "It's all of a dollar-ninety plus tax, and that's including the potatoes. Just think of it, a meal for two."

"Really," I said, looking back to the shot of Diana Ross in a Cadillac.

"Here," she said, beckoning me with her hand, "you can sit here." She slid a serrated knife over to me and I proceeded to slice away. I could see the taste buds there and pushed deeper into the muscle. "This smells good," I said, looking around the table at the salad, plate of mashed potatoes, and bowl of brown gravy. I took a bite of meat, then potatoes and chewed them together.

She waited for my response, and I smiled. There was a radiant glow to her, like she had done this great thing. She was sitting with good posture and chewing with her mouth shut. Aretha Franklin was singing about getting a little respect, spelling it out. We sat cutting our food and eating a good meal pretty much in silence. I could tell that she was preoccupied as her eyes were tense and shifting.

"How's school going?" I ventured to guess that that might be the reason.

"Next week are midterms, so I'm just going to have tonight with you, okay?" She said in a round-about way, slicing another piece of meat, taking a bite.

"That's okay, I know how it is. No distractions to break the flow of logic," I said, finishing up my portion and wiping the last of the gravy with a roll.

"That was good," I said, taking my plate into the kitchen.

"I'm glad you liked it," she said, getting her plate and other dirty bowls. "Why don't you put on some other music."

I put on an album from the Rolling Stones and turned it up. *You can't always get what you want*, reverberated in the room. Jan glanced out from the kitchen and smiled, as I turned it down and got her by the hand and pulled her out where we danced in the living room just beside the stereo. After the song ended, she went back in and to finish the dishes.

Another song came one about Ruby Tuesday, *who could hang a name on*, and I went in and stood beside her as she plunged another plate in the suds. "Here," I said, "Move over and let a pro show you how it is done correctly." I had to smile at my joke as there was a ring of truth to it. She smiled too. I finished and she was over by the stereo putting on an album.

A slow song played, so I dried my hands and bowed, to which she curtsied, and we held each other and got into the rhythm of the song, my check against hers, feeling the silk of her face so close I had to shut my eyes. This street-wise girl from Watts and this farm boy from Paonia, Colorado. An unlikely pair linked to the song *Crimson and Clover*, by the Shondells. Her touch was like a magnet as we swayed and moved against each other. I listened to her and thought about the meal and what it said about her. I wasn't ready for the responsibility thing—the one thing that I was sure of, but I was arguing with myself to keep the options that were open, wanting my cake and wanting to eat it too, without even letting on to her that this was running in my mind we continued to dance.

We turned out the lights and morphed into waves tossing and heaving to the pull of our tides in the night through all the secrets we weren't sure of, that we took for granted ,holding our breaths deeper, until we gave out and our dreams found us each on our own distant shore that went on and on.

Look Out Below

The next morning light broke through the blinds, casting bars sideways with the tinkling of chimes and the rustle of bushes on the windowsill.

"Cliff," she said, "Why don't you take the car and come back on Sunday. That way I can get in some study time, and you can have fun."

"Sounds pretty good," I said, getting the keys. "Thanks," I said, turning back and giving her a kiss and a hard hug.

Having a car hadn't even occurred to me, so it took me by surprise, as I drove off checking the gas gauge that read about one quarter. Pulling into the flow of the traffic, taking a left up at Saint Michaels. Coming up to Alameda, I took a right and headed east until I got a parking space and left the car there.

I headed past shops bustling with tourists. I sat on a bench at the square and watched it take life. Time slides easily on the square as its motion keeps your interest, with different kinds of people to watch and theorize as to what country they might be from due to their dress, which along with their body type, complexions, and facial features made a game of just sitting on this bench.

Towards late afternoon I got tired, just about the time Buffy came by. He had his girlfriend, Maferd, from the Santa Clara Pueblo under his arm who had a friend that had beautiful dark eyes and a sleek slender body.

"I gotta ride," I told him, trying to impress, to which he said, "Oh yeah, sure." It took me a while to find it, as I couldn't remember where I had pulled in. He was beginning to doubt, when I saw the gray dull finish under the tree. Walking up, I pulled out the key and opened it and then got in.

Buffy slid in with Maferd and her friend along side of me in the front. "Hey, let's go up the ski basin and see what's going on there," he said.

I wove through the narrow streets to Hyde Park Road that turned into route 101 ten miles out when I looked at the gas gauge. By this time, it was getting dark. "*Crap*," I said out loud, "we don't have enough gas, gotta turn around." We turned back and headed for the glittering lights of the main city.

As we came to where the snow was getting less, Buffy motioned to me. "Hey, I'll show you a short cut," he said, and I pulled over. He took the wheel and we went about a mile or so, where he pulled off on this dirt road that suddenly went steeply down toward the blinking lights of the city.

"Hold it, Buffy," I said, catching sight of a washed-out section just ahead.

He stopped and I got out and could hardly believe what I was seeing. Ten yards ahead, the road had washed out and fell straight down. I put a rock in the front of the front tires to keep them from rolling down. Seeing that it was too steep to back out of, without chancing a screw-up, I had got to get a tow truck.

"Buffy, I gotta go a get a tow truck. Wait and I'll be right back," I said. On the main highway I quickly caught a ride back to town. I got off at a gas station that had a tow truck parked way in the back.

"What would you charge me to pull me out of a place where I'm stuck?"

"Twenty," was all he said, and soon we were heading up Hyde Park Road to that crazy turn-off that Buffy had chosen, which I recognized. I couldn't believe how stupid I had been going along with his idea. When we got there, Buffy was nowhere around. The tow guy hooked up and pulled it from its perch from what could well have been a tragedy. All the way back, I was just glad Jan hadn't been along for the ride. I had pushed the envelope far enough. I drove to her place and put the keys in the ashtray, left a thank-you note, and took off.

Sunday night came with me thinking about the Pantry Restaurant, so I turned in early so that when that shade of gray came around in the sky, I'd be ready to hit the pavement down Cerrillos. I got there with time to spare to get the water in the two sinks just right. I got into a steady rhythm as dirty dishes started rolling in. The flow was there, the clues were present, seeing humanity in the eggs, oatmeal, or eggs, which preferences mothers leave with us *ad infinitum*. In the back of my mind

Jan's presence floated in my thoughts and how easy it is to get lost in the silk.

The Phone Call

When Ruth the head waitress yelled, "Cliff's got a phone call," it sounded like it came with an order of pancakes. It jolted me loose, immersed in the mechanics of cleaning, pressure to be applied and keeping just enough economy of motion so that I was in a smooth grove, allowing my mind to glance back over my interlude with Jan. I was on top of my game and ahead of the rush, which allowed me to see I was ahead enough to take time-out for the call.

"Ah, hello, Jan," I said, recognizing her voice, "Huh?" I said, trying to hear her. Her voice was tight as she was speaking fast, spitting her words out. She was mad and her words were coming at me fast like a machine-gun. "Where'd you go that night? What'd you do with the car?" she said. "Did you let Buffy drive? I found sage brush jammed under the bumper. I want to know, no, I have a right to know," she said, coming to a stop.

"Ah," I said, stalling for time to get thoughts together for defense.

She sensed a lie was coming and cut me off, "No, I want the truth." What could I say? The truth was worse than a piece of sage brush, so I did the next best thing—I said nothing, and it got more and more awkward. The silence became more accusatory than had I come up with an outright lie.

"Well," she said after what seemed like a long time of sustained quiet. I was hoping that something would break the impasse, but the more and more the moments ticked off, the more it looked like it just wasn't going to be.

"Well, then Cliff," she said with a measured sense of precise declaration, "let's forget this whole thing. If you can't be honest, then that's it."

The phone clicked to that busy signal and I stood there numb as a stone. I hung up the phone and headed lifelessly at half speed to the dish room.

"Let's pick it up, Cliff," Linda said, noticing quickly my lethargy of movement. From that time on, it was all downhill, you might say, as nothing went right. A fork prong poked a hole in my glove, and it filled quickly with scalding water. Finding the place where the fork had poked a hole in my skin, which stung and reacting to it, I turned, bumping saucers that clattered to the floor. The boss poked his head in and measured the damages. The bottom was finding me as the drain did remnants of people's breakfast with the pieces of pancakes, eggs, bacon slices, oatmeal chunks, or toast, all gummed up in the metal cup with the holes in it, that fit on top the drain.

Humpty wasn't doing good right now, in his soaked apron—back two steps.

Free Falling

Funny how point A and point B don't necessarily have to be related. It's about what comes next, even if two plus two doesn't always equal four. It's all just a state of mind, I kept telling myself as the ache went on. That's not to say that that phone call started me drinking, but it helped, as I already knew the brown fluid could make it seem better than the things were. Smoking pot got you paranoid with police showing up out of the blue, so I spent my time inside, looking out that side garage window.

The end of winter brought its storms that came, went, melted, froze. The snowdrift behind the front fence arched over soft pale white.

Suddenly, like a caged tiger, I had to make a break, and I put my coat, breaking through that snowdrift where it had gathered on the sidewalk, the caged lion was getting out.

I went toward town to see who I could bump into by chance, hands in my pockets, my bread bag around my belt, the notebook inside.

CHAPTER 25

Blind Sided

All this was still raging inside that wouldn't let me go, like I was suddenly on this stormy sea cast with waves that came and went with recriminations of what I shouldn't have done and how stupid and a loser I was. I wasn't in the mood for the square, so I opted for the quiet library, up the brick steps, past the bulletin board, rentals, roommates wanted, to a poetry tonight ad done in Norm's unflappable over-the-edge style, done with a simple bold magic marker on a yellow folded page for the right effect to hold your gaze a bit longer.

Walking by, I glanced at the door and coming out, I recognized her from the ER (the nurse who I worked with at the ER who told me about Campho-Phenique). "Hard day at the ER?" I said, to see what her response would be.

"Yes, Cliff, yes, it was one of those days that sneaks up on you after it's over," she sighed. "How have you been? We miss your enthusiasm." She added, "A suicide came in late in the shift. He was about your age. Just don't know any more. He sliced himself up right through his wrist. He lost a lot of blood. We pulled him through, but it was close."

I shook my head at the tone of her voice as much as at the description.

"He went into surgery to get tendons sewn together," she added.

"Lucy, he was lucky to have you there on the blood pressure cuff," I said.

She sized me up. "You've lost weight, Cliff." Then she glanced toward the door and back at me, "Take care, you're looking ragged." With that, she headed toward the door down the long red brick steps.

I laid out some magazines to search for articles to consume my mind and occupy thought. The articles ran in front of my eyes without lodging conscious impressions. A story of the Mommas and the Pappas wandered around, and one on how Michael Jackson's dad was a real slave driver. I walked out, realizing I was wasting my time fighting it.

I just had to go where the flow would take me and count on my resolve to pull me through what may come. That found me leaving, heading south toward the square and diagonally across it on the shoveled sidewalk west towards San Francisco Street, hands in my pockets, hearing my shoes crunch on the snow that had fallen since the last shoveling of the city's sidewalks.

The coffee house was on my mind, going by the shops and the movie theater. I was on automatic pilot and was glad I had that steno book in my bread bag. There were poems in it that I was wanting to hear how they'd sound. I reached out for the doorknob, turned it, and quietly walked in, found a seat, and listened as Norm was in the middle of a poem.

She held me and the night went diamond black
Nor did I ask more of her than she volunteered
Which as sleep found me and left me again

190

Divided the night with silk sighs and thunder
Running headlong into this gentle steel blade
That cut me leaving all I could do to hang on
Her name was Ann, Ann of a thousand reasons
All of which made me clay in her working hands
Unasking beyond my words she listened for
So giving, poor as I am, made me king of mere
This price far more than gold but I would
Even if your smile or touch hadn't found
Til the charging bulls of my stampeding self
One by one ran into oblivion silk and disappeared.

As he spoke, I could feel the power as his voice radiated feeling and the words glowed with meaning. It woke up a feeling inside of me that I had one I needed to read. I reached for my steno book and found the poem, scanning to be sure it was ready to be read. I'd been fooled before thinking one was, only to find out it wasn't. Being a fool, hearing your words paint a bunch of gaps hurts bad. To try to pull it off, as if there is something there, hurts worse. As I glanced down, I could see that this one had real potential. Taking that risk, being out there, is what makes poets come alive.

Norm had been observing my keen interest and, knowing well the signs, he said, "Let me introduce Cliff Alexander, one of our poets, he's got one he wants to share with us."

There was a scattering of applause as I headed toward the stand. "Norm's right," I said, "I've got one. It's called *Ode to a BIC pen*."

It is to you in this long night, that I
In my wandering sight write you thus
Which roll these syllables into words
Rhymeless working in the meanings

191

Always you between me and oblivion
Out of your loyal point streaming
Here among all the premises at once
Not the least of which summoned
Through these ransomed times
Consumed in those long moments
You were my friend for thirty cents.

Long upon the snowy streets outside
My notebook on her kitchen table
Or café counter, all that I am or was
In the pages like some cat in the alley
That only meant me surviving beyond
What I could discover in the moments
Not knowing most of the time myself

Behind the black ink curling into letters
All that on this page could cut free
Syllables for wings and out of my mouth
To fly in this veined lisp images of life
Grit and thirsted breath ungiving up
Among all the threads that can weave
Into being out of this my chanced dream
If but this BIC were all I could ever be
Then drowning here in these images
Must, between the silences, yearn I
My heart through you.

I stopped and for the first time I felt the acceptance didn't matter. In the silence as I read, I could feel the connection grow deeper as there has been a quiet hesitation of movement—a deep listening, almost a holding of the breath as the words had flowed, images. There was a lingered power that stayed, after I stopped reading. I stood there and the applause did come, and I took a humble bow, knowing that the reaction was to the words, independent of me.

I glanced over at Norm and saw that he too was applauding me, which I didn't know how to react to, since it hadn't happened before. It made me feel warm inside to know that I had touched him. I sat down and felt relief, as if a weight had been lifted off me.

I looked around, to see if David was in the back somewhere. Not seeing him, I have to admit something went out of me, as a compliment from him would have helped. Still I wanted to hear the way he said the words that seemed to push me so and touch a part that made me want to go where I hadn't before.

I hung around but without David there was something missing. Norm felt it too, as the other poets that came and went. He glanced around as I was and not seeing him, kept glancing. I was ready to leave, when Norm came over and held my arm. I hesitated feeling the strength of his grip, he said, "Good poem." I glanced back and felt good, going outside into the cold night.

Nothing for Granted

The next day I was hanging out at the square, as the sun broke through and sent clouds of steam up off the plowed streets that showed asphalt absorbing the infrared and sending the warmth sky ward in the haze. The motion and the breeze, as well as the people who were out, each had a rhythm of its own. Yet together there seemed a melody, and catching the moments just right of life opened a crack in the blue sky and broke free my feeling of hibernation, so I felt I could dance or sing or catch what vision I could.

As Buffy came by, I looked down at his shiny boots. They were black with a buckle on the side with a strap that tightened. "Traded them for a leather necklace I wove out of rawhide," he said, looking out into the distance, allowing me to get a good look without making me have to feel that I needed to make a statement. "Tonight, there's going to be a pow wow. I just may dance," he added.

Always for some reason, he left a degree of uncertainty in a statement, which was the Apache way of saying that if it was meant to be in the scheme of things, and if nothing got in the way, then he'd be there.

I responded, "I'll see if I can make, so I'll see you." (I was beginning to get the hang of how to respond to a Mescalero Apache).

Getting out of Santa Fe can be a good thing after a while for a change, to get away from the we-are-the-intelligentsia-of-the-world attitude. Hitching on the road can be a lot like pen in hand with a poem coming where juices flowed like magic, projecting with my thumb, facing the traffic, feeling the currents grow, watching the cars come and go, knowing there was someone in the fates that I was meant to meet, as a pickup slowed and pulled over to the shoulder of the road.

I opened the door and a Spanish song blared out. I slid in and sat down. "*Ay yi, conto a mio*," hit me full blast as I shut the door. We went down lava hills south of Santa Fe past the Santo Domingo turnoff, then by the San Felipe turnoff with the Rio Grande to the right, folding down like a silent shadow velvet over the rocks with swirling currents and eddies. Down beside the alfalfa fields of Bernalillo and Rio Rancho in the distance, toward the oncoming spread of blinking lights that sprawled in all directions. Albuquerque was fast approaching as we fell in with the flow of the traffic.

"Where you going?" he asked, "Close to the university as you can get," I said. "You know that university that's west of town, University of Albuquerque."

He downshifted, pulled off the interstate and up the ramp, slowing down. Then pulling to the right, he shifted back up and went north about a mile. He took another right and went back east, as the lights below spread out like a universe below us, blinking full of neon.

"I used to drop my daughter off here for night classes," he said smiling. "I'd drop her off and pick her back up all that year. Was worth it. She got her nursing degree and now she's got a good job." He added, "So, you can see this is giving me flashbacks," as he pulled up to stop.

I got out and said, "Thanks a lot."

I walked by a parking lot where a security man was trying to direct the pickups that drove past, oblivious that he was trying to help. Inside the gym the drummers were already getting warmed up. *Ka bum, ka bum, ka bum, ka bum,* the large drum beat out with four guys hitting it. Dancers were prancing around in a counterclockwise direction, warming up, beads flailing, feathers moving to a blur, dancers spinning, keeping the beat. Now and then each one would take his turn, bursting with creative energy, going into a spontaneous sequence of spins and pirouettes raw with power, only to blend back into a more steady routine of movements and spins. As they did, they seemed not to touch the floor, gliding in the rhythms.

I got a Pepsi and settled in, waiting for Buffy to show up and do his thing. One of the staid-looking girls caught my eye, wrapped in a Pendleton blanket. In the procession the young ladies were steady as they plodded doing a two-step, while the guys would freelance full of twirls and reverses. Suddenly the drummers would pound harder and then stop to take a break.

I could feel the pull even though I didn't have a fancy get up to join in. The head drummer signaled the last go around. Buffy hadn't showed up yet, but people were getting ready to leave, putting their stuff in bags, gathering kids, and taking off their feathers. I hit the bathroom and when I got out, the place was empty, so I went by the student union and saw a student leaving.

"Say, could I get a ride into town?" I asked, with pleading in my voice.

He gave me a slow look and motioned, "Sure, hop in the back."

I got in the back, right behind the cab towards the center—the best spot where the sweeping wind would be least, with my hands in my pockets. Down the road and on to the highway we worked through the traffic. I was in a bad way, my chances of getting a ride next to nil, hitchhiking at ten o'clock. When we got to the Menual exit, I had no idea what my plan would be. I had no place in Albuquerque to crash at and was just getting over my cold and watching my breath cloud up in the air. after he pulled to a stop, there was a complete awkwardness as I got out and stepped away.

"Thanks a lot," I said, turning toward the lights from where the city lay. *Ah, what do I do next?* I glanced around from the bottom of a gentle slope. From there, I could make out the top of buildings in a mall. To the right, I could make out the silhouette of a steeple.

What do I have to lose? Heading up the short steep grade, I visualized that I might find a warm safe place to crash for the night. As I got closer, I felt how important this eventuality was. I turned the knob and the door opened. I walked inside the chapel, found a heat register, lay down over it, and drifted off to sleep.

The dreams ran in tangents and disconnected segments going all over—until the light broke through the stained glass. I heard a door open and the sound of footsteps on the hardwood floor. I sat on one of the pews trying to seem as normal as possible. Little by little, other people came in and sat down with sober expressions. As the organist started playing quiet thoughtful music, I got pensive. All the motion and the voices in my mind suddenly stopped going, and the words to *How Great Thou Art* took shape in my mind.

The pastor began the service, announcing a potluck dinner later, and then the singing and the sermon. At the end came a call to testify. I found myself getting up and going to the front right below the pulpit.

"Do you confess Jesus as your savior," the preacher said in a serious tone,

"Yes, I do," I said with tears coming down, feeling humbled. He put his hand on my head and said because of my belief that I was saved. I sat down on the front pew while we sang another hymn, which song became a blur as the sequences of my life came flashing by with the notes of the song, associating events I had no control over.

Then the service ended with a prayer and people came up to shake hands. "Like a ride to the potluck?" one of them asked, to which I nodded yes, and soon I was among good-natured strangers eating a plate of chicken and potato salad, feeling that odd feeling about how I had gotten here.

When I saw the pastor, I thanked him for leaving the door open that gave me a place to consider my messed-up life. "By the way, thanks for leaving the door open, that really saved me," I said.

He looked over at me surprised and said, "Huh? We don't leave it open."

It wasn't until they dropped me off at the Bernalillo Turnoff that it hit me, as I faced the oncoming traffic with my thumb projecting a positive image. Tears started rolling down and I sobbed, trying to keep my composure as best I could, not wanting to miss any ride that might be about to happen, the way it does, as my emotions gave way to the reality at hand. My ride was coming. In the corner of my eye, it pulled over as I ran to it, drying my tears.

"Going to Santa Fe," I said, sliding in the front, glancing at the driver.

"Really appreciate the ride," I said, as he picked up speed, shifting to fourth. It was middle afternoon when we rolled in and up Cerrillos Road.

Ah oh, no

When they dropped me off at the St. Mike's intersection, I headed for Norm's. I took the turn and crossed the driveway, up the steps, and knocked.

"Come on in," he said, opening the door and going back to sit down. "Where you been?" he asked, putting his hands behind his neck.

"Went to a pow wow in Albuquerque; just got back," I said, looking around.

"You sure put a lot of energy into that stuff," he said, looking out the window. The New Mexican newspaper was on the table, so I found the place that Norm had opened to the headline of a suicide attempt. The name David Goldstein hit me as I scanned the details.

"Did you read this?" I asked in disbelief, as my eyes raced through the words.

"*Crap*," Norm said, "Why did he have to do a stupid thing like that for? How much money you got?" he asked, pulling out his wallet and looking in it.

"Let me see," I said, pulling out what I had in my pockets. "Ah, five dollars."

"With my eleven, we've got enough to give him a visit," he concluded. "What'a you say we go and cheer him up some? A couple of poet buddies."

CHAPTER 26

Here We Come

As he drove, I thought back to the conversation that I had overheard. "*Crap*," I said, remembering that I never had got around to tell him.

"What?" Norm said, keeping his eyes on the road ahead, navigating.

"I overheard a conversation his girlfriend had with two guys dressed in dark suits with Ray Ban's that federal agents wear."

"Yes, and I painted *Whistler's Mother* too. Don't get carried away. Why would the Feds want to mess with him anyhow?" he asked.

"Well, he was a sniper in Vietnam and he killed a lot of people there."

"Plenty of people got killed there. What's that got to do with him?"

"See, they gave him pictures of people to kill; some were civilians. He was a sniper. He still has them in a cigar box. I saw them when I was over last time."

"Hum," Norm said squinting, going over a narrow bridge and up a hill.

"He told me he'd get this picture and a contour map with an X on it, and then, his Boy Scout map-reading and hunting skills took over. He loved that when he was on his own; he was free, he had freedom."

"Hum," Norm said, downshifting for a hill, "A guy like David having that on his conscience, could be what would push him over."

"That's not all. He told his religious mother he was just a cook the whole time, and he's afraid if she finds out, she'll see that he was lying those years."

"You knew that, and you didn't think something like this could happen?" Norm asked.

"We all have lies going on. You just fight for the space to work them out," I said, as the white lines multiplied, coming up from the winding darkness. Now and then a car in the opposite direction would break the blackness. A silence enveloped as we rode, sensing what was at stake with David. It was as if he was out in deep water and we just couldn't get out.

"You're right, Cliff, we each have our own phantoms we must wrestle." Norm said, as the sign came up that read Las Vegas Mental Hospital

Here Goes

"These places always scare the hell out of me," I said, as we slowed. The guard, seeing our lights, got up from where he was sitting.

"Don't worry, you and me are harmless crazy people," Norm said.

The guard leaned out of the shack with his flashlight shining into our eyes.

"We are here to see a friend," Norm said quickly with impatience, looking back directly in the guy's face, who then lowered the light.

As Norm pulled forward, he glanced, saying, "I'm not good faking it. I smelled pot. A stoned guard, hassling me? I don't think so."

We pulled into the visitor spot and we headed for a door at the end of the sidewalk. Inside, a hallway led up to a window where a nurse sat looking out. She set down her book and picked up a black pen. she slid open the window, adding, "How may I help you?" She was easily in her middle twenties and on the thin side. She reminded me of a nurse in Ft. Carson that I liked.

"We're here to see a patient called David Goldstein," Norm said.

She pushed the logbook over, Norm signed and pushed it to me where upon I scribbled my signature. She said, "Follow the yellow line on the floor."

The yellow line led up to a room where we heard voices as we got closer. Gilligan's Island was on, and the captain was speaking. An orderly stationed near the door quietly walked over to us.

"We're here to see David," I said, and headed where he had directed us. Sure enough, I made out his ruffled hair, as he watched the TV, something inside of me took over, and I walked up to him and tapped him.

"David," I said, as he looked up at me and in slow motion recognized me. He looked over at Norm and smiled and gave us a hug. He wore a blue bath robe with white slippers. His right wrist was taped.

He held out his left hand, "Sorry, the right one doesn't work too good. I cut through all the tendons, trying to get to the good veins." He said seeming to run out of breath before he ended his thought, whereupon he sat down.

202

"*Crap*," Norm said, searching for the right word, waiting on David.

"Shit happens?" David injected wryly. "I feel like shit for killing those guys, Susan couldn't understand that, I already tried talking it out with the shrinks in the Army. That didn't help either."

"But," Norm tried, "we're friends. Talking to us would've been different."

"I thought about it, but then things got confusing," he said, trailing off and looking back to the TV, as a gorilla came at Gilligan.

Norm and I glanced at each other, thinking the same thing. This was going to be over our heads, as something had gone out of David. His voice didn't have that ring to it; gone too—that chip on his shoulder.

He glanced up, "Luckily, I write with my left so I didn't screw that up." David ambled out of the TV room and took a left to a room, where he slowed down as we followed him. I glanced in a room by chance, and there was Lucero, the crazy Spaniard from the library.

I stopped, surprised, about the same time our eyes met. "Senior Cliff," he said, "Why are you here?" Come to visit Lucero?"

We shook hands, and right away I saw that the defiant look was gone. He had a new resigned look like a fighter that had been beaten. After our handshake, I expected him to blurt out his side of the story, but instead, he said, "Wheel of Fortune is on. See you later, we'll talk."

David came by and said, "He's telling everyone he's a big landowner."

"He is," I said, "it's true. I met him at the library just before Christmas."

Suddenly, I noticed there was a spinning action in my head, and I looked for a chair in David's room to sit down and get some balance. As

I did, I followed Norm's voice asking David questions. David reached under his bed for an envelope. "Here," he said, "Read it, if you get a chance." I folded it putting it in the bread bag, then hooked it back under my belt. He smiled, "Still got your bread bag, huh?

David yawned and stretched, looking across the hall. "See that room is where we play ping pong," he said. Then something inside me crashed and I got a claustrophobic feeling like I had to run and get out, but I held position and sat there. We listened to David in a silence that he would have filled with insight. I waited for him to make a comment that would set the moment on fire about how the place was run or a personality defect run down of the nurses—but nothing was coming except a narrative of his day's schedule of activities.

Finally, after watching Wheel of Fortune, Norm looked at me and we both nodded. It was time to go and we both shook David's hand. "Thanks for coming," he said, and I felt like crying but gave him a hug instead.

The Trip Back

"It had to be the downers," Norm said, starting the engine. "Downers keep you in the now, shut off everything else. I had friends in Frisco who would get their allotment on a monthly basis. They'd keep meticulous schedules so that they wouldn't run out and go cold. It's almost like chemical surgery where you cut out a personality by default."

Norm said, "Game shows, looking outside, lunch, meds, becoming a spectator for life. I'd think about breaking him out of there, except he may be over our heads. When people snap, that's how we're all like Humpty when he had his fall." He turned to me with a sad look, "What a waste."

We drove in quiet, still shocked what we had just witnessed. Finally, Norm broke the silence, "You got to let it go, Cliff, or it'll pull you down. You can get sucked into a whirlpool that you'll never get out of. I've seen it. Okay, David got a bad shake. You and me both love him and his poetry but," his voice almost broke, "we're going to have to let him go, and see how it plays out on its own. Probably wouldn't hurt to say a prayer."

I was too confused and unsettled by all of this and had nothing to say. I had thought when he saw us that he would've snapped back to normal. Skips of my days in the stockade and the trips to mental health came back. I'd found safely apart from them, after all this time, but I was sliding; that was, until I drifted off to sleep with the white lines coming back at me.

The next day at the dish room, I had energy and was in the flow pretty good. Breakfast plates, cups and saucers, dried-on egg yolk and dirty silverware had me connecting with what should come next to keep the sequence going. That was, until I had to take a leak and glanced in the full-length mirror.

I started crying like a baby until I had to look away and go to the sink where I splashed cold water on my face til I stopped. But every time I tried to leave, another spasm would hit. Finally, I got all cried out and my gut was tired, so I left and finished up my shift and started my trek back, past the pawn shops, north, toward my apartment.

CHAPTER 27

Mary

I walked past the St. Mike's turn-off, not wanting to stop. Before long, I found myself on Canyon Road heading for the bar. I walked in and sat down, ordered a whiskey and a coke from the bar lady. While she got it, I checked the juke box and put a quarter in. *All along the watch tower people kept the view* broke the silence. I got the drink that was waiting for me, tipped it back, then swallowed, feeling the slight burn go numb down my throat, and then to my head. I felt someone's hand around my arm and saw Jason, the painter/carpenter from the commune. He had one of those I-just-got-to-show-you-something looks on his face.

"Here," he said, "I vant you to meet someone especial," grabbing me by the shoulder, so that I followed him. There was a young lady with blonde hair at the bar, sipping her drink. He took me so that I was to her left as she turned around surprised.

"I vant you to meet Cleef. Cleef, dis is Mary," he said as we shook hands, not knowing what else to do, and he vanished, walking into the back room. There was an awkward drop-off in energy as we both fumbled for words.

"How long have you known him?" I asked, glancing into her pretty face and noticing how her hair shined in the red neon light, as it did on her face.

"Oh, about four years. He's a good painter. A little off, but harmless," she added, looking at me.

"Maybe that's why he likes us," I said lightheartedly, seeing a delicate toughness in her eyes, as she turned and looked ahead, taking another sip from her drink.

She added, "Good one," smiling back. "But are you harmless? That's the question."

I leaned back as she ran her hand through her blonde hair. The supple skin of her neck shone in the dim lights as a few strands fell back. She yawned, our eyes met, as she sipped her drink with the red straw.

Rollin, rollin on, came out of the juke box, *proud Mary keeps on rollin.*

"I just can't get away from that song, it's everywhere I go," I said, wincing.

"Maybe someone's from the Delta here," she said, "You write?" she said, looking closer at my steno book with its raggedy, beaten-up cover.

"Sometimes, when I feel like it. Words are my vehicle, they save me," I said.

In the background, a band was warming up in the side room, hitting chords, and the clatter of someone on the drums tuning up, and finding the rhythm that got closer and closer to coming into a semblance of a song I recognized.

"Testing one two, testing," the guy at the mike said with background clatter.

"Want to dance," I asked, offering my hand.

She nodded, "Why not," and took my hand with her drink in the other. We wove our way in the darkened room, around the tables and chairs. About the time we reached the dance floor, they began, *Hey Mr. Tambourine man, play a song for me, I'm not sleepy.*

Feeling the beat right off, I glanced and she smiled and followed me, which rhythms seemed to unlock the tensions I'd been feeling. I found a certain power that moving to the drum beat generated in me, both an intensity and freedom in the rhythms, *in the jingle jangle morning.* Moving to the music connected me with this person Jason had found. I leaned over after the song and said into her ear, "My name's Cliff."

"Yes, I remember, Cleef," she said, not giving me much to go on, but enough to say that she was positive. A slow dance came up. As we got closer, I felt her hair tickle my neck and her slender body move with mine, as the rhythms worked the spaces.

Out of the Blue

Some winding was going on, moving back and forth hesitantly, finding like two magnets adjusting their opposite poles to mesh better. If I was falling, I couldn't tell, since everything around me was in slow motion except for her eyes. They seemed to find something inside of me as the music swirled around us and the dim lights gave us a sense of privacy. Even though we'd just met, there was something comfortable about her as if Jason had been right, about the hunch he had for us to meet like this. I had a feeling it was so right, at the same time something was scary not knowing anything except that I was going to find out where this might go.

208

Closing time hit, with me not wanting to hear that it was the final number. As the lights came on and we squinted awkwardly, holding each other in a shared not-wanting the chanced meeting to end way. With us wanting more, we grabbed our coats and followed the crowd out into the cold night air, with our breaths clouding up in front, arm in arm, unaware of the pressure we both held each other as the crowd dispersed and we were left alone.

"Which way are you headed," I asked, her looking at her as she looked away. With her free hand she motioned down the street.

"Mind if I," I started to say and felt her squeeze my arm, interrupting. "No," Mary said, and we fell into a pace that both of us kept, going arm in arm. I could see our breaths mingle then disappear with the air as we walked by adobe houses that had been there centuries. We went past a grocery store and right up to a driveway, turning in as we crunched our way up in the hard snow. I heard the jingle as she pulled out keys and fumbled to get to the right one. After finding it, she carefully slid it in and turned it clicking the door open.

The door swung open and Mary and I stepped in. As she turned on the lights, a small living room came into view. A sofa, table—a phonograph on it, and prints of paintings of a lily pond hung on the far wall.

"Want a cup of tea?" she asked. "Could you turn on the stereo? It'll take a while to warm up. I put off fixing it since I need music, and it could take a week. I don't know what I'd do if I didn't have music to get me through the day." She took my coat, laid it on the sofa, and went back into the kitchen.

"I know what you mean, music helps me over the rough spots too," I added, thinking back to that burger stand on Cerillos. "I don't know how many times I've played Junior Walker?"

"So, you like Junior Walker? she asked. "Yes, he blows a mean saxophone." She offered me a cup of tea with grey steam coming over the rim, "I put honey in it," then she sat beside me.

The sweetness was right, enough, but not to take over. I could feel warmth spread from my stomach, relaxing me. "I was pretty cold," I said feeling the warmth spread from inside.

She turned, "So was I," and put on a record by Paul McCartney that had a picture of cranberries on the cover. It was an easy-listening song with a samba beat and a beautiful melody.

As she turned from the stereo, I put down my cup down. She smiled as I reached for her and we danced to the music. The speed still wasn't quite right as the turn table hadn't fully warmed up. We recognized it at the same time and smiled at each other.

"I think in winter, the warm-up time's longer," she said, leaning back.

As the speed got normal, we swayed to the easy beat. The wind was blowing and a branch rubbed against the window outside. I could feel her there, pulling me with the same force that I was pulling her.

"Just a second," she said, going to the kitchen. Coming out, she lit a candle and turned off the lights. The candlelight lit her face, as she came back. She smiled with her pouty lips and her cheeks that rounded delicately. The candle flickered silhouettes on the walls, us swaying back and forth. You could hear the wind got stronger, as the branch jostled around harder.

Somewhere in the middle of the song our lips rubbed against each other almost by accident, except there was a magnetism that held them together. For such a slender lady, the force with which she kissed was almost fierce. We stopped dancing and kissed with the wind outside and the music inside. The soft candlelight flickered beside the window as the wind buffeted cracks and made a strobe-like effect that gave a slow-motion quality to our embrace. Snatches of impressions came in between—her eyes half shut, that slight smile, a sigh, each like strings to a violin that were being drawn by a force beyond me turning against, then going with, compelled by the next note, playing it by ear.

Soon, we found each other in the night, playing notes silently with our touch so that falling was never so good or loosing track ever so sweet, I lost all track of time and only wanted more, as if this thirst was growing each moment within both of us.

In the morning she had to leave early to get to her job so she left me a note. When I woke, it read, "See you Friday. I have a busy week. Mary."

The week had a new beat to its play, as the dish room took on a new feel. Even Margarette had to admit my energy was first class as she ducked in and wiped her hands on the towel, and left with a smile on her face.

The perfume Mary used kept coming back like an old song that you can't quite recognize, but that keeps coming back over and over, and part of that zest included the fact that Thursday night at the café was coming up. Time flew, until there it was, with me looking through my notebook checking out poems, to see if the images held, and the transitions stuck without leaving the listener wondering what the heck I was saying.

I pulled out my Rainbow Bread bag, opened the notebook to a poem, and out fell the note David had given me, back when we had visited him. I remembered him saying, "Read it if you get a chance," in a nonchalant way.

I opened the letter, "Dear Cliff, I never thought how time goes when you're penned up, where all you can do is sit around killing time. I'm not cut out for this, even with the drugs I'm getting, it's not working. I slit my wrist to show Yvonne that I couldn't live without her with me. The intensity of my love seemed to do just the opposite to her. I really miss your visits and us reading poetry like we did those times. I'll bet you're at the coffee house right now reading this, got you, huh?"

I smiled at his insight and thought how we're alike, as I had felt that way sitting at the Hepatitis Ward back in Fort Carson that seemed so long ago. Yet we weren't alike, as I had a selfish streak—I always looked out for number one.

David's letter went on, "Funny how boredom sharpens your sense of vision. I see you like this brother that I never really had, but would've liked to. I still think a lot about that poem about your Dad sitting at the depot. Would've been nice if I had someone like him that was waiting for me. Hey, I included a poem I'd like you to read for me since this is my reality and that's where they come from, huh? Give it your best shot from me. I'll be thinking about you, and know that you'll sitting on the right side near the wall hunched over your poems. That's what I miss the most."

Norm came on in a somber mood without that humor and one-liners. He glanced over at me, and, I could tell he wasn't over David's plight. I gave him a nod, he nodded back and proceeded reading one of his own

There was something that was missing in his delivery—his enthusiasm. He finished, bowed to acknowledge the applause, and sat down.

I had to get up there and read David's poem. I owed him that much. I unrolled it and took a deep breath and gathered myself, thinking this was best to read it cold turkey, so to speak, without prompting, so the words could work themselves just as they came off of the tip of his pencil.

David's poem

Sometimes there's one that takes over the time
And sometimes they're too many and they blur
Pulling away, running together, images stampeding
Then just like that, or it all can stop without warning
The combinations don't hold like they did before
But I just can't tell just what it is that causes it
Like I can go only so far and then it goes blank
Back down through them once more to get it going
This time, I think that I can break it clean then begin
Like I'm running and I can't catch up to my shadow
Me and the ceiling fan keeps going round and round
Watching Gilligan and the captain solve a problem
Then I go back to where I'm trying to find it again
And I can tell I'm close but the words don't come
And I see that I've gone and lost my place again.

It was hard reading it as I saw myself in that hepatitis ward waiting, not knowing what was going to happen next with my gut hurting raw. The prisoner of boredom unable to break out, and that's the scary part. Boredom eats on the only thing a poet has that's worth anything, which is being free to go way out, way past the limits others will keep, so that oblivion becomes the default alternative like getting drunk comes from the alcohol. But the feeling doesn't stay on permanently the way bars on a jail cell can do to you when you stuck there in place. I sat down, happy the lights were coming only from flickering candles since I needed privacy, as I saw a lot of myself in the poem. In a lot of ways, that poem was from me in that hepatitis ward. Only, he said things that I didn't even know were going on but were.

Moved by David's poem, Norm walked over to the mike. "Ah," he stared out, his voice cracked and he got quiet. Standing tall, he went on, "I didn't really have a clue what I was doing back in the fall when I started out this poetry reading thing." He added, "I knew the poetry thing, was around it plenty in Frisco, but I've found out I really had no clue about the power it would have. What I am trying to say, is that I'm learning to take less for granted than before. I'm dedicating this poem to both Cliff and David."

Norm's

Words on a Thursday night flying high
Going for broke on the tight rope walking
This part in here that knows no other way
Words opening vistas look out here we come
Falling or soaring all at once sheering edges
So, for this way but once I had to let it go go
Midnight or haggard morning matters not
For you, yes, just for you alone in this night
Which weave these words held of heart string
More than meager I could fathom on my own
Doth bind and wind alike as breath lends life
For the images speak for themselves wound
Just so in the meanings that can't any other way
The poet's mark which makes him nameless
As nature knows not but truth to give up secrets
These lips to be ever what it may take to say
Give of bread and a vagabond's fortune
For this reach that holds us all in these words
So that we are never again the same.

He stopped, hesitated, and looked out to us from the podium. There was something in the moment that stood out unique, even with the nobility of the way he had spoken the words that were uncharacteristically absent of any of his spontaneous flair, as he stuck to the script of his poem that dictated his emotions. He bowed meekly, completely out of character from what I was used to seeing.

I doubled-checked to see if my poem was ready, and thought it's now or never.

My Poem

Velvet fire goose bumps and stuttering
You there and me trying to get it right
This night black upon our eclipsed skin
What's left for me to create of nothing
Pulling rabbits out of hats to entice you
All of my conscious efforts to show
This connection I'm feeling's all I've got
Without saying it, there, I can't hold back
What this touch is worth I can't believe
Loving you is so easy free and so far out
Giving up secrets without even saying
Falling smile glance skin sigh unmattering
Smooth for the time relatives this fast
All or nothing is really thoroughly alive
Where this next comes down to you.

I stopped and held the silence standing there, allowing it to stand like brandy is savored before it's swallowed, then savored again. I didn't need the applause and gave it no heed as I wanted to share it more than I wanted the appreciation or the acclaim of it to be liked. Writing about love was new to me, and maybe I wasn't so good at it.

CHAPTER 28

Mary on My Mind

Next morning the dishes flowed much like Norm's poem had last night. The corner of her face and the way her eyes closed like oval sculptures and the glow off her skin in the candlelight flashed, here with the pots and pans, and allowed me to expand the dimensions of my limited dish room.

This king with latex gloves and damp apron, leaning over the sink, singing along with the radio, "*Wild thing, you make my heart sing, wild thing*." Some part magnified and part in the zone, feeling the lulls and surges in charge of the exact nature of the cleaning. Time skipped with the dishes and the roll of the steam off the top of the rinse water, swirling designs.

Punching out at four and walking up Cerillos past the pawn shops, going straight for the shower, and then feeling the heat roll off my body with the steam-up smell of Dial soap. Getting out and drying off, humming any song that came to mind, looking in the mirror, still seeing that I had it—the cheekbones, the color of my complexion, my intense eyes. Not dwelling too much, just enough to get the grove

HIPPIE MEMOIRS: SANTA FE DAYS

going, knowing that I was bringing something that surpassed the usual, giving me confidence as I put on extra Aqua Velva.

I was forty minutes from Mary, knowing the way already by heart, going over it countless times in my mind, finding the shortest way, taking narrow streets. Still noticing the uniqueness of their construction, how they found a way to make the most of their patch of ground. I felt the air grow thick with the cold evening coming on. My pulse kicked up as I made it to the gravel driveway and started up . My mouth was getting dry as I got closer to the door, thinking of what to say.

Three's A Crowd

I could hear voices, one of which was hers and the other guy's. As I got there, I took a deep breath and knocked, and waited. A stocky Indian opened the door and looked right past me, going on by. I'd seen him around town and heard he was a sculptor and was good.

The gears inside my mind started working, my thoughts tumbled toward to a gap.

"Come on in, don't mind him," Mary said, pulling me inside.

I still didn't know what to do, as my concept of being the only was gone, but I still walked in and projected calm as my heart was still beating hard.

"He thinks he can come by any time he wants, not anymore," she said. She put her arms around me and held me tight, her perfume wisp enveloping me like a silk cloud redirecting my thinking so that I quickly forgot about him. Her skin was against my cheek, and we kissed and the spin started.

"Let me get my coat, then we'll get going," Mary said, pulling away. Out into the night we walked,not caring that it was cold.

When we got to the dance floor at the bar, it was already crowded and the band was charged up and in the groove, cranking out energy We slipped into a zone and fell under the spell of the sound, counterbalancing and connecting in the beat, making eye contact, with bodies rubbing in all directions, feeling the excitement grow, we saw just each other.

After the dance was over, we sat at an empty table. A nerdy-looking guy came over and asked if he could dance with Mary. I nodded my acceptance and watched. I could tell he liked her, by the way he overdid his movements, trying to make more of any possible connection than what was there.

It didn't bother me, since I was the King of what I saw and expressed. Mary was mine; even if the old lover couldn't let go, my time was now. She came back, sat down, and I ran my hand over hers and squeezed. There was electricity in our touch, and that was all I needed to know. We danced more, feeling the weight of the beats to move between as I always did, as if there was something else I was needing to feel that all-out-nothing-left, complete getting-in-the-beat sweat coming down, where the music became me. Moving to it broke any barriers I felt, which was in a way how I could be alone. Yet being with Mary gave me a light feeling.

We left after a couple more dances and made our way back to her place. We acted like moths to foreign light with a deep hunger for more. Sleep found us under the blinking stars that heaved to a different force. If light was silk, then my sense of touch found all the shades of a rainbow.

Saturday morning found us figuring out to head over to the square.

Penguin's Studio

We wondered to Penguin's studio and climbed the stairs. Buffy was there working on leather, intently braiding it to make a bridle. Penguin was working on a mural-size painting, intense as ever. He glanced at me and gave me a nod of recognition, as did Buffy. Both of them went on with their labors, giving me a real compliment that I was not an intruder in their private world that they'd created. That made me feel I'd accomplished a great thing, as this lone Anglo was being accepted by two unique and uncompromising people.

I put my arm around Mary, and we lingered over Penguin's artwork. Mary looked at me and said, "Where's the bathroom. I gotta go." I glanced in the direction of a hallway. She left, glancing back as Penguin kept concentrating on his work.

Buffy came over to me. "You know, she doesn't love you like you think," he said in a matter-of-fact tone and then went back to his leather work. He glanced up and looked at me as if he was looking right through me.

About that time Mary came back and took my hand, "Can we go?"

"Hey, see you," I said. "I'm going to see what's happening at the square."

"I'm going to be dancing tonight at Albuquerque, if you can make it," Buffy said, giving me eye contact. "I'll see if I can make it," I said leaving.

I felt embarrassed at Buffy's remark, as I thought this was real because I came alive and felt great with Mary, as the time with her hand in mine made everything else a poem. The poetry was immediate—all I had to do was to work the images a lot like Buffy was doing, braiding that leather into a bridle, although in my case feelings transferred into the words that made transitions that flowed and were seamless.

Moving On

"Cliff," Mary said, as we crossed the bridge near Alameda Street. "I need you to understand something. Jason, that guy you met would come over anytime at night he felt like, and I didn't like it. So, can we make a rule that you won't be dropping by after one o'clock?"

"Sure," I said, "rules are good. They keep away misunderstandings." Great, I'm making headway as we crunched over the drive and went inside, stretched out on the bed, and watched the shadows from the trees, that ran arms on the wall as if they were wrestling.

I glanced at her clock and thought of Buffy dancing at the pow wow, which I hadn't had a chance to see, and it was time to leave. She was soft like Mercury, as my hands ran over the contours of her lips. I kissed her, thinking of the time it would take to get there, and I could feel that I just had to go. "I'll make it back tonight after I see Buffy dance," I said pulling away.

To See Buffy Dance

It took all my strength to pull myself from the force of Mary's scarlet lips, getting my breath. I put on my coat and gave her one last long look, and soon the gravel under my feet pushed out. I was off feeling the forces as the sun slid to the west, grazing the clouds, turning them orange and then lavender that rode the pinks, swirling pastel. It was meant for me to go, and the rides would come as I stuck out my thumb. I could feel it, as the excitement was there out of nowhere like the sunset that was now going purple and faint red so that I thought I could touch it.

The rides fell into place to the Bernalillo turn-off and to Los Lunas, where I got off and hoofed it to the university auditorium. I stood in line and found a good seat where I could see the whole swirling show that was the pow wow.

Smooth as Raw Silk

220

Buffy was easy to pick out, with his bony elbows and herky-jerky motions. Even with the sliding glide to the *boom, boom*, I could easily tell that his style was uniquely his. Similar to the others, sure, but still much apart like he was in his own world, twisting and turning, ever keeping the beat. He was all angles of elbows and legs like he was suspended over the floor, coming down to keep the beat pure, changing direction at the last minute, spontaneous moves bound to a completely unexpected next turn in motion. Even if I hadn't known him as a friend, I would not have missed him out there, as the dancers came around in their own way, challenging him with intensity or twisting a break. But his smoothness, coupled with a sure herky-jerky, last-moment spin would draw me with his I-don't-give-a-crap approach of flowing motion, like he wasn't fettered by what might be expected—it was in his blood. A Mescalero Apache with nothing but what he had out on the floor.

"*Hey ya, hey ya hey, hey ya*," the singers went along with the drum, as the drummers slowed. Buffy accented finality in movement like he was putting that exclamation point to what he'd put on the line. Then, just like that, it was over and he stopped and stood still.

I could see him glance in my direction, as the drummers were starting again with a different song. There was that distant look like he was seeing past me into the distance to a time long, long ago that stood still and froze me in my thoughts. To his vague nod, I nodded back to something that had stood there, still as you do when you don't want to break the spell of the moment's life. Just like listening to David read his poems, so that you held your breath as the moment moved on. The drummers got their rhythm and heaved into another song.

The dancers came alive again, spinning and ever reversing their paths. I had seen what I had come for and felt a glow from how Buffy had danced. Somehow, that whirling had been meant just for me. The odd Anglo that could connect across the lines with a Mescalero Apache.

221

I hurried to the bus station, thinking of the silk of Mary's skin in my mind. I could not shake the impression of her silk on my skin. At the bus station, I found I had just missed the nine o'clock bus. Which meant the next one would leave at twelve and would put me into Santa Fe at one o'clock.

Crap, I thought, remembering her request not to visit after that certain time. As I rode on the bus, my mind kept going over what I should do, thinking more and more like Cinderella. That empty feeling stayed in my stomach right until I got off at Santa Fe. The argument stayed with me, twisting and turning as I wrestled with it, feeling that pull to be with her so strong but still not wanting to mess up. That phone call from Jan was still fresh in my mind as I hesitated in front, but turned and headed towards Norm's place to play it safe, with no guts.

A lady answered the door. "Norm," she said, "you got a visitor." Norm came up and leaned on her shoulder, squinting out into the dark. I could tell that my timing was way off the mark, as I made my way inside.

"Were you at the Canyon Bar?" I asked, finding a seat and plopping down. As I did, it hit me how tired I was, putting out all that effort to see Buffy.

"Yes, me and Barb made the scene. Pretty good band," he continued.

"Did you see Mary there? Thin with blonde hair?" I asked nervously.

"I did," Barbara said. "She left alone and looked a little disappointed."

"Let me guess," Norm added, "You were at a pow wow, just got back."

I smiled and tried to hide my embarrassment, feeling I had screwed up.

222

"You can crash, if you want, we're pretty much done in, going to sleep," he added, pulling her close. "So if you want you can curl up over there." Norm turned the lights off, and the place was full of snoring from both. They were in sync as Norm snored followed by Barb, as he took a breath.

So many things were spinning in my head that it was hard to slow it down. Part of me wanted to go over to Mary's and knock lightly on her window, just in case she'd be waiting for me, and the other part was against it. I'd already screwed up with Jan out of stupidity and didn't want to again, during which time there was a razor in my gut that was turning slowly. That was, until four-thirty when all at once it felt as if it had been severed.

The ache stopped, and I got scared. I waited until the dawn to go over, but by the time I got there, all I found was the note Mary had left. It read, "Gone to Taos to see my godfather. See you when I'm back. Mary." My mouth was dry as I reread and read it again until I had it memorized.

CHAPTER 29

On The Ropes

Part of me died between those written lines that got completely lost. I turned and walked out the gravel driveway by the grocery store. I made a right turn toward Alameda, hands in my pockets. I hunched over as snow fell and could feel melt run down my back, symbolizing to me how my life was.

I had no place to be and felt no reason to lead out in one way or another with no direction. I just got through another day, a listless person going and stopping, waiting til Friday rolled around when I could see Mary again and hoping that I could patch up this big misunderstanding between us. But knowing something had bled out without any reason to explain away. The other thought was the one that got me through the week of grey days, so that with a sense of apprehension, I headed up that inevitable driveway and knocked on the door, heard footsteps coming inside, and held my breath as the door opened.

Mary looked out and said, "Come in and warm up. I won't be able to stay, since I'm going skiing, I gotta get ready," busily gathering things into a bag she was filling.

I wanted so bad to hold her but she wouldn't slow down to where I could. "What about putting on some music?" I said, sounding as casual as possible. Walking toward the table, I reached for the album and got the record out, awkwardly finding the hole in the middle, ready to put it on the turn table.

"Cliff, there won't be enough time to warm up before I gotta go," she said.

A sigh went out of me as the sound of tires crunched on the gravel outside. A generic- looking guy came in with an expensive down jacket and Ray Bans.

"You about ready?" he said, grabbing the bag that she had packed.

"Cliff, this is Stanley. Stanley, Cliff," she said, "What'd you hear about Taos?"

"They got another twenty-five inches," he said, the bag in his hand.

How can this be happening, echoed in my mind with an out-of-sync feeling. I stood by the door, and Mary gave me a kiss on the cheek to usher me out. I stood off to the side, waving while they drove off.

All By Myself

And then, like that, I was by myself, feeling this rip in my gut go deeper. I ambled to the street and walked past the corner grocery on Garcia Street to De Vargas, over the little bridge west on Alameda. As it started to snow, I felt like the only person in the town, hands in my pockets and my head down, my chin tucked under my collar.

What's wrong with me, began as a little refrain in the skipping flashbacks. If I could have stepped out of my body then, I would have—I was disgusted. One foot after another, I went back to my apartment and lay on my bed.

Dishwashing was drudgery now, as there was no inner glow to radiate. I moved like a robot, locked into the routines long instilled in my head like an autopilot dishwasher. Except as I turned, I forgot the stack of dishes I left there, and they fell crashing, porcelain pieces flying in all the jagged directions. I cut myself badly, picking them up just as the boss poked his head.

"Cliff, here," he said, reaching for a band aid that he put on the cut.

"Thanks, Mr. Alexander," I said, as I felt that somehow he was concerned

That night a hundred times I went over, wishing that I had gone over to Mary's, even if I would have broken her rule. *Crap*, I thought, *why didn't I?*

After the shift, I went up Cerrillos past all the landmarks I knew so well and only half- checking the lights at the St. Mike's intersection, I went on, almost getting to the other side when tires screeched hard. I turned to see a pickup missing me by inches, which I didn't much care about. As it continued on, I saw Buffy in the back but didn't even give him a nod.

Smelling the burnt rubber, I stepped onto the sidewalk and busied myself looking at the designs weather had left in the sidewalk with the scent of Chanel # Nine in the back of my mind like an old song that I couldn't forget. I made it to the gate, to Mary's apartment, walking in. Friday came and I had to go and see if there was anything left for us.

Point of No Return

As I started up the drive, I saw her sitting with one of her girlfriends, talking. I got closer and summoned energy, "How'd you ski trip go; you have fun?"

"Yes," she said, smiling at an inside joke they had as I walked up. She glanced past my look, determined not to respond.

"Well," I said, my mind going blank with the awkwardness between us. I kept waiting for her friend to excuse herself, as I stood there hanging on

"Then," I added, "I'll see you around." And I left over the gravel.

That afternoon the dishes stacked up but I was determined to work, still going through the motions, but now that zombie feeling was gone. I was pissed off that I had tried but she had pulled that hurt-wing crap. After work, I wandered over to the post office to see what had come in. There was one written in David's handwriting with my name just legible.

David's Letter

"Dear Cliff, thanks for coming out with Norm that evening to see me. I got a favor to ask of you, since you'll understand and will know why. You know that I told my mom that I was a cook while in Vietnam. Well, I don't want her to find out about the assassination-sniper thing. Would you go to my pad and get that cigar box I kept those pictures in? I'm worried a reporter might get a hold of them and make me his way of getting famous by writing my story for the public. It'd make a good story—I had a sixty-thousand dollar bounty on me. Anyhow, I wrapped it in aluminum foil and buried it in the fireplace under a bunch of ashes, so it should be there since my rent is paid up and it doesn't run out until next month. So what'a you think, Cliff? Help out the last wishes of a poet friend, just for old time's sake. I'm not afraid, since I have this good plan that came to me last night. I remembered that moment I squeezed off a round and it came clear. You're a good friend, so I know that you will come through for me. Don't worry about me, I'm in a good place and that's what matters. Take care, love David," it read.

227

As I reread it, I got an empty feeling; but at the same time, as I left the post office, I knew what I had to do. Still, I was torn, since if I did his request, that was saying goodbye and I'm not good at saying goodbye. So I walked around the streets looking for a way out, but nothing came except images of the town, which in my present predicament, were all disjointed with no tie-ins.

Toss the six pennies, check the *I Ching* like at the commune. So, I did the next best thing, I let it slip from my mind altogether. Since it was Thursday, I thought about going to the library to read. The light was already sliding to the west, the shadows lengthening along the ground with a colder breeze coming off the mountain. Walking had become a way for me to sort out, minus the boredom. I found a pull inside grow that said there were words that needed to be brought to life, and that edge brought a thrill, which gave me hope, and a new force came into my striding. With the crystal air's sharp impressions, I walked quietly home and the slanted shadows the streetlights threw to the ground. I made it there and lay down, letting the events come back to me and realized for whatever reason, too much had passed—it was gone. I feel asleep, in a flat-line dreamscape, going smooth and easy.

CHAPTER 30

Words like Friends

I was jerked awake with the thought of Dave's voice on the poetry night. *Crap*, I thought, I've probably gone and slept through my chance to read. When I got there, there was a new buzz in the air—a feel of excitement. I went in the back and sat down, relieved I hadn't screwed up after all.

That night at the poetry read, Norm had brought in an old friend of his who was a jazz musician that played the flute with a loose jazzy style. His name was Lennie. As he played, time stopped still for his notes. Sometimes, he held it or allowed it to transition into a whole new set. His melodies were contagious how they were structured as they flowed and were blended like a theme does to a story within the paragraphs.

He was good, the way he could hold that note and then pivot right then out of the blue, and bring that melody softly back before you knew it. It was magic, and I was captivated by the adroitness that he exhibited, much the same way David was with his voice. Only Lennie opened paths that I never thought existed before that made sense and held the vision that you could almost see, but not quite, except that it had to be there.

Lennie was a slender man of medium height with thinning hair, and as he'd play, he'd bend over as if his flute was too heavy. All else seemed secondary to the wings that his music made. An idea stirred in me that I pushed down, afraid of falling. But the idea wouldn't let me go and kept coming back stronger than before, and my heart kicked in, beating stronger so I had to go with it.

Ah ha, the idea became clearer, and I figured what I had to do. Lennie had an approachable way about him, unlike most musicians who would have that better-than-thou vibe about them. So, I waited until he was done with his set of music and had sat down while this other guy came out, playing his saxophone similarly.

I could see why they were together, as their styles were much alike. I took a deep breath, wandering over to where Lennie was relaxing. "Hi, I'm a friend of Norm's, and I'd like to try something with you. Your music does something to me, and I'd like to try to make poetry while you play, and see what happens. That is, if you'll give it a try?"

He rubbed his chin with a pensive look, "You know, I like it a lot." He added, "Let's give it a try. I'm always up for something new."

I was elated and nerved out at the same time—scared, you might say. I had to go backstage and walk around, pacing back and forth by myself. I saw Lennie go over and talk to Norm, who was nodding as he did.

When the saxophone guy was done, Norm came up to the mike. "Max," he looked over, "not too bad. It's good to see that some things improve with age, huh?" giving him a wink, which indicated an inside joke. Then he turned back, looked at the audience, changing expression. "We have an experiment of sorts that we're going to try out on you. Lennie and Cliff will be mixing poetry and jazz to see what'll happen. We'll call it jazz-oetry."

Norm's bow was our cue to get out there and see if we could get it done. I took a deep breath, and looked over to Lennie who started with a sweet note that he let go and then went on a run of his own. The words came to mind as he played magically in a complete line. (I'm going to call it *Water*)

Water

Nor did it matter that life was not sure
That each day scattered out meaning less
As the seasons scolded the ground white
Our breaths mingled on the edge of the breeze
As we held hands and your pulse moved mine
Lennie went on and ran a series of runs that changed in tempo and
came back around to that melody he had found.
While you candle lit the apartment barely
Past midnight silken shadows around us
Became dragons of our sheltered terrors
Going closer to what we feared the most
With the light flickering around the room
Which thirst that would not let us go
Deeper in the silk we both fell free falling
So that nowhere else seemed to matter

Lennie went mellow and took a darker tone down an octave, staying there, trying to go back but repeating the sequence. He broke through and found faint new beginnings of another melody coming noticeably there, almost not. The sensitiveness with which he brought it softly back made me go deeper where it'd been out of touch in me.

The whispered words first showed shadows
Thought all I thought of was this gentleness
That could open all that I'd ever wanted

231

So my heart mattered not, for promises
Would hold even after you said good bye
I knew our love would pass this hard test
Freedom's seal would prove none other

Lennie's playing got intense, as he let more gap in his notes and made them almost like a whisper so that you had to listen, coming back to that theme but not too clear, still just barely.

When you came back I couldn't help
Looking at the waxed tangle on the sill
With your eyes glancing out the window
That was framed with soft white powder
Not even when the razors struck hard
With the way you said those words
Aloning me cold and out of balance
Did I believe you—no not then either
Twined that silk could hold me like steel

Lennie brought the music back louder by small increments, until it was back, taking its place louder than what I was saying. Now there was a conflict between the words and the music, which dynamic gave the conflict I was feeling with the words—even more of a conscious extent that I could feel inside that made me have to dig deeper and come out hard with them.

Hazy out of focus streets crossed
Curbs hurdled going back out of sight
Little by little my whispered thoughts ebbed
Hands in my pockets my head bowed
One step after another that not then either
Did I believe you
He stopped and let go and stood there waiting for me to continue.

Child whose pain fathers you older
Upon these thoughts full of gone

And then he broke in, interrupting with his intensity blowing hard, changing altogether the melody into a totally new one pulsating, which made me stop and the words would not hold back.

Which time spans you to memory
You who seined my life with fire
But fear whose dragon slayed you fair
Must inherit while thus entwined
My lot when time was young
And loveundefined.

Lennie now blended the old melody somehow with the new one and let the notes go softer and softer until there was only silence. We both stood there while the audience applauded with feeling. He put his hand on my shoulder and nodded, that we'd done it. With a smile on his lips, he turned and bowed to the audience, which I did following his lead, as I was new to this, and awkward too.

As I sat down, I was feeling exhausted elation, and sweat was pouring off Lennie's forehead. Norm slapped me on the shoulder, shook Lennie's hand, and said, "The whole time in Frisco, I never saw it done so good." He added with excitement in his voice, that told me I had done good.

Golly, I felt close to Lennie, and I didn't know him, which was odd, but I couldn't help it, so I hung out awkwardly, sitting there exhausted. There was a gap in the action when Lennie seemed to regain energy.

"Thanks," I said, holding out my hand, which he took and we shook.

"Hard to explain," he said. "We were lucky tonight; that's all I can say."

Other poets read, but something had gone out of me. There was a clean feeling that I was a different person than before. Still the same guy basically, but not downcast or depressed anymore.

New Water

The next day, soapy egg yolks and dried-on bacon scoured evenly, the porcelain went squeaky clean, stacked up on the shelf near the lazy-susan. I was back with the flow of plates, silverware, cups, saucers, and the radio. The day was back, filling with all sorts of possibilities one thought might make. By the time I was done, the zest was back and my rhythm was good.

CHAPTER 31

Take Not for Granted

I wandered up Cerrillos by the shops, glancing at my reflection and saw that rainbow-colored wool hat pulled down over my ears; my hands shoved into my pockets, my shoulders hunched, my collar up and my chin down, with a steady stride.

On to the rough weather-worn sidewalk, glancing at what was left of the day, I figured I'd head over to Norm's, not slowing down. "Come in," he said, hearing the steps squeak. "Went good last night with Lennie. You had something going." He said taking a swig of wine and wiping his mouth, "But we got some bad news, and I'm not good with bad news." He looked at the opened newspaper on his table.

I found the headline and scanned right to the one that read Mental Hospital patient takes own life. I raced through it, wishing I wasn't reading til I got to his name. *David Bernstein is survived by his mother in Lawrence, Kansas.* I got numb and the room began to spin so that Ilooked down at my shoes and the worn-out gray tile floor full of scuffs. "Oh no," I said in a small voice, feeling weak and folding the paper, numb with shock.

"*Crap*," Norm said, "I didn't think he'd do it. I just don't know." He added staring at the table in disbelief with a glassy vacant look. He took a deep breath, "The funeral is tomorrow at ten. You were right, he was a sniper over there in Vietnam. Had a sixty-thousand-dollar bounty on his head, dead or alive."

"Golly, Norm, I gotta go for a walk. Got to do some thinking," I glanced back at Norm who nodded. I had no idea where I was going; I just kept walking east by houses toward town, where I found a park near the post office. I whimpered, between the thoughts of what I recollected. It didn't make any sense for him to give up like that, *no sense at all*, kept ringing in my mind with snatches of his ruffed hair.

I leaned back on the picnic table and looked at the sky, closing my eyes, and I thought about his letter and suddenly, I knew what I had to do for him.

David's Errand

The sun was down, by the time I got to David's house, shadows had disappeared and blended into the overall darkness. Evening was leaving the darker forms of trees and deeper indentions of the ground that I could just make out if I took my time, thus slowing me.

Something told me to go behind the house and go down that hill behind since the house may have been watched by those guys with his old girlfriend. A feeling that something wasn't right kept me finding cover of trees. I made my way behind the house down the hill that I remembered had risen above it to the east. I made it to the house and slipped around in the door right beside a pile of firewood. His ax was where he had left it.

My eyes adjusted to the space inside, remembering how it looked when I visited. I went by the table and chairs, remembering when we shared poems. With the poker leaning beside the fireplace, I probed in the ashes and bumped a hard object and worked it toward the front, where I could get a hold.

Sure enough, it was a cigar box wrapped in thick aluminum foil. Just then there was a distant sound of a vehicle coming up the road, crunching through the frozen puddles. *Crap*, I thought, looking at the large box he used for the firewood. I quickly gathered the wood and getting in, I put it back over me. Then I got still, as the sound got closer until the vehicle stopped, and the sound of doors opening and shutting broke the silence. Footsteps got closer and the squeak of the door opening, and muffled footsteps on the floor came in.

My heart kicked in high gear, as the scuffing sound came from the floor, and I could see light of a flashlight getting pointed around the room. "Something's different," the voice said, "check there, see anything?"

"I don't see anything different. Your sixth sense is wrong again," the other voice answered as they poked around inside and stopped.

Just then a mouse rattled through some papers right near my head. It was all I could do not to jump up to get it off me, but I held position. Like David's poem, my breath went in then out like that reed in the water.

"Hear that?" one voice spoke, as the mouse made a break for it.

"I sure did, and look, it's a mouse." the guy laughed. "You're wound way too tight. Let's get out of here. I've got a steak and a waitress waiting for me at the La Fonda. Your problem is that you don't know when to stop," shining the flashlight around one last time, and then they left.

Footsteps headed toward the door and the sounds got distant with vehicle doors opening and closing, engine started, and the sounds the tires made got smaller going off down the road, until I was sure that I was alone. My heart pounded like crazy, my head still resting on a log.

Stalked

I waited a bit and when the silence stayed, I got back up, clutched the box and slipped outside and back up the hill. About halfway, I stopped to catch my breath looking back down, and just barely visible, I made out a dark form going toward the house. He got there and went around, and took the direction I had gone.

A cold feeling hit me, and I started out again, this time much faster. I hit the top of the hill, picked up my pace, and I ran. I could pick out the breaks in the trees that I could take. To my left was a ledge just above a steep slope. Suddenly, I thought that might be a good place as I could go faster. I stopped to be sure that I got a good look before I committed myself to that route.

Then I heard branches crack, where he'd stepped on a dead limb, and a wave of fear swept over me as he was gaining on me. Then a movement caught my eye, and I veered around a rock. A hand reached out, grabbed me, pulling me into a cave. I saw Buffy's face, as he put a finger to his lips.

His presence surprised me, as he had white paint on his cheeks. He motioned me to follow from the direction I had just come. The way he moved without showing any effort impressed me. I found it hard to stay up; he was walking on rocks so that he left no trail, which I tried to do, making me go slower. We got up the hill where he squatted down near a cedar tree.

"What's in the box? You robbing a friend?" he asked seriously.

238

"No," I whispered, as I caught my breath, "Just pictures." Now wasn't the time to explain. "What are you doing following me around anyhow?"

"Someone has got to look out for you. You almost got yourself killed back at that intersection. I tried to tell you that that girl friend of yours was bad medicine. I tried to tell you. Anyhow, we got to keep moving, put distance on your tracker. Come on," he said. We worked our way into a deep wash whose vertical sides covered us, until it emptied into a riverbed. Then we kept moving over the large river rocks, leaving no trail at all to follow.

The slice of moon light gave just enough light to see the next set of rocks. We got past a bend in the dry riverbed, pulled into a grove of cedars, and stopped sitting on some rocks. I was breathing deeply.

"What's in the box?" he glanced at me.

"Photographs of people David killed in the War. He was a sniper. They kept coming back to him, and he wanted to be free of them." I said, leaving out the part of David's death and lies to his mother.

Buffy got serious and offered to take the box, which I gave him. "So, he wanted you to bury his ghosts?" He took the box. "You must be a good friend."

"You're a good friend too," I said. "You really saved me tonight."

He listened to what I was saying. "I will do this for you," looking at the box. "The Apache way." And he left.

I could see the lights from Santa Fe. I followed that direction and came out on a county roads that led into town. As the town got closer, I felt good inside I had kept a promise and had got done with what I had set out to do, even with the help of my good friend.

239

David's Funeral

I woke up and put on a clean pair of Levi's, my favorite clean shirt, and headed south toward the cemetery I'd gone by many times. It was a sunny day with the blue sky already lighting up turquoise, undercut by feather-like cirrus clouds.

I went in the wrought-iron gate and saw a group of people ahead. Buffy was under an elm tree with his usual stone face expression. As he handed the box to me and took off, without saying a word. Up the gravel road I could see Norm where a scattered group of people around a grave. I couldn't help but observe what a strange group of friends David had, all of whom were unique and as much of an outsider as he had been, which was a compliment, that he had lived his life quite simply.

True, he had been a hero, but still chose to have a regular burial, wanting to keep it from getting much notoriety, knowing his story could really gain a life of its own and spoil his wish to keep it a secret. As I approached his grave, memories came in disjointed scenarios. I remembered the clear way David's voice had sounded reading at the coffee house when it was all so new and scary, and our chats and poetry shared at his house, and our crying by the fire.

I took a breath and walked over toward Norm past a dark sedan. Just then, two guys in dark suits wearing dark Ray Ban sunglasses got out, and got right in my way. "Excuse me, I need to see that," the larger one grabbed the box. As he opened it, turning it upside down, ashes scattered to the ground. He smiled as they fluttered, catching a breeze that had kicked up. "Oh, how clumsy of me," he said, giving the cigar box back to me.

240

Norm shrugged, as if he didn't know what was going on. I walked up, both of us still in shock. We shook hands and turned. Norm also had sunglasses on too—the kind I had seen at Circle K.

The ceremony was getting under way as the priest addressed the throng that gathered. "The Lord giveth, and the Lord taketh away," the priest motioning with his hands to people around the closed casket, including David's ex-girlfriend, who had on a dark dress and glasses. Her countenance differed from the rest. She was distraught, shaking as she sobbed deeply, ready to come apart any moment. On either side were two men in their dark suits.

I couldn't help but to go back to that scene in Romeo and Juliet when the king says at the end, "All are punished, all are punished."

The ceremony ended and the people broke off one by one. Soon it was just Norm and me and the guys shoveling the dirt back in. There was nothing to say, as we watched the dirt pile up on top. "You need a ride back in town?" he asked, to which I nodded, walked with him to his ride. I got in and leaned back, glancing one last time to the grave. I rolled my window down and watched the trees, sidewalks, cars, houses, people all go by in a carousel way.

Norm started muttering, "*Crap*, there's no letup," as he shifted up to third gear. I glanced over, surprised to see the look on his face go to anger. "Someone broke into my place last night, while I was sleeping. They took my stereo and my good typewriter. *Crap*, and that electric typewriter cost me fifty bucks too." He shook his head, as he continued to navigate the intersection.

"After all I've done for this town. It just isn't right. It just isn't. So I figure, since this is the last week of the month and my rent will be due, so," he went on, "that last day will be when I pack up and leave. I'm out'a here," he added with a sense of finality.

Hold on, I thought, as scenery went by, things are going too fast.

"You really liked David, didn't you?" he said, after a long pause pulling up to the parking lot in front of his place.

"Yes," I answered, "we were different, and we were the same"

"You know, none of this has to make sense, but some of it does. You saw things in each other due to your love of poetry and life. That is our gift. Life, to a poet, is an adventure searching for truth in his vision. It's just too bad how life can pile up on some of us, so that we think there's no other way out than ending it. The words we use to describe what we find gives us power. David did not die alone, even though he did; he will live on in how he affected us, how nothing'll take those nights away when we read out our souls together, trying to get it right. If we are true to our life, the way David was to his reading, our epitaph won't need any fancy words to dress it up. It will have happened," he said, getting out going up the steps.

I got out, walked over and saw the broken window.

"I'll see you on Thursday night. It'll be the last poetry reading," Norm went inside and I headed toward town.

Farewell Night

Norm came out relaxed, and it was apparent he had moved on and that he held no grudges from what life had thrown at him. His form was back as he reeled off his *Cadillac Poem* with gusto pell-mell, still that bull-in-the-china-shop of social expectations. Let-her-rip wasn't the style of Dylan Thomas or ee cummings but it was his. It was authentic as he read his poetry with zest.

"Got a fresh one," he said, and his mood turned to somber. He stood there, waiting for the audience to catch up to the change as if he

242

was a surfer, waiting for that moment the wave breaks for him to make his move and he began this time holding back.

Norm's Last One

They say this won't work and that's it's way too old
You know, the mechanic shaking his head at your car
With those greasy hands completely covered in brown
You can see it in his eyes how much it's going to take
But you see something that he doesn't see there
That little glimmer there—you gotta be quick to catch it
When he was young would've been all he'd'ave needed
And he stopped and held out his thumb and index finger close to
show the space that he was talking about for dramatic effect.
Going back under the hood you could catch it there too
Body language doesn't lie, he's saying there's hope
So I said before he straightened up, to give it a shot
And I peeled off fifty dollars to get the ball rolling
Like waiting on a friend getting open heart surgery
Reading the magazines with the sexy girl on the cover
In front of some souped-up car with flames on the side
Going over all the engine specifications and raw data
Giving the mechanic the space he needed to find it
Which link had broken down in the vital sequences
Lingering in the advertisements of friction preventers
All the time hoping his hunch had been the right one
That would get me back down the road with confidence
That the next dot on the map was going to get met
So that when he came out of the garage greasy dirty
I didn't need him to say a word from the look of his face
I knew the click had found its place—he'd fixed it
And that it was meant to be for me to be on my way
Close-but-no-cigar kind of a deal but just enough for me.

Norm stopped and bowed slowly that was meant for all the nights he'd read his guts out loud, sharing the most personal of changes, and had been the catalyst for me and David to discover that fire. I found myself applauding long and hard that drew attention to me, but that's what can happen when you get caught in the moment—another lesson I'd picked up from Norm that I was now part of me.

It got quiet with the sprinkling of conversations ebbing and flowing. I took a deep breath and it was now my turn to jump in. My heart was beating loudly *kerthump, kerthump*, as I adjusted the mike, as I tried to compose myself. My mouth was dry, dryer than usual, and I was hoping the wheels weren't coming off. In spite of myself, the words came out, "Here's one called *David.*"

David

You were just so sure of his claim
That he was staking in the images
Coming from the syllables rich in color
That it was there more than ever
In the same words you'd heard before
Only this time they were different
Some royalty had entered the room
And had made them rich in sound
As if for the first time you heard them
Pure as they were always meant to be
That true C note all violins are tuned to
That exists in just so few of us here
But when they mix in the meanings
That longing in your heart unlocks
So that all you know is what is being said
All else—even your very best is suspended
As you want not to miss even the smallest

Whose slender power is just that in you
That missing piece that is waiting to be filled
Of slimmest of chances it's all that it takes
Upon this here and now you'll see it clearly
And then it's gone in the pure sound of it
Holding on to how that sound thrilled you
How one fire can kindle where there wasn't
So David, we bid you farewell this night
For what was not to be we must admit
Remembering the best that grew our souls
On those nights we left our aloneness
For the caring place your words filled
We bid you this most quiet night farewell.

A nod from Norm at the end was all I had needed as I took a bow. This time it wasn't for myself, it was for David and his memory.

Some Help For Norm

On Saturday morning I woke up early, thinking of Norm and his stuff. Heading over to his place, I took the worn-out shortcuts, easily going through the place where the wire had worn from the post. If you bended and twisted halfway, you could slide through, and then down the alley past the large grey dog that knew me by now, and only perked up his ears until he recognized that it was me. Then I went to the fence that was the south boundary of the parking lot where Norm's station wagon was parked, side door wide open with boxes piled here and there in a jigsaw-puzzle manner.

The car was already sagging to the end—the springs overloaded. I walked to the open door about the time Norm poked his head out. "You're just in time," he said, going inside and pulling the sofa away from the wall adding, "Here, get that corner," he said, bending over.

I got a good grip and we lifted at the same time, out of the door down the steps. We hefted it gently on the car roof. He threw a nylon rope over to me, which I attached to the mirror and threw it back to him. He grabbed it and tied it to the opposite mirror.

Back inside, it did not look much different, except for the grey worn linoleum in front of the gas heater looked smaller without furniture. There was no stopping Norm, as he already had the route down, and how long it would take him to get to Austin—his new spot. "I got this vibe about Austin, and I can't get it out of my head," he added, "Grab that chair and put it up on the end of the sofa."

Soon, it was all stuffed or tied on. I was caught in the middle of my emotions, not wanting to let go.

"Hey," he said slapping me on the back, "had some good times, huh? I'm going to remember you, Cliff, and what happened here." He gave me a hug and I hugged him back. Then he was gone out the gate to the apartment complex and down the road.

True to form, he was like a lion heading down the highway in his Ford Falcon station wagon, looking for what might come next. I couldn't help but keep waving, until he turned down Water Street and I lost sight of him ,still picturing him, shifting up to second gear, and, like that, I found myself alone, in the middle of the parking lot.

CHAPTER 32

A Secret to Share

I wandered over dusty streets to (you guessed it) the plaza, letting the experiences I had shared with Norm come back. On San Francisco, I headed east, seeing the buildings coming up. I worked my way through the morning shoppers that were busy going out of the tourist shops with a full range of mementoes.

I got a bench at the square and watched the eternal Frisbee sail back and forth. I saw Gabrielle with a group of friends, laughing and joking around. I caught her eye and got a momentary stare back, punctuated with a nod that caught me off guard. Over my head again, I held position.

After a bit, she broke from the group with a friend, and came over and sat down. Golly, her face was alive with color and her dark eyes shone clearer than I had remembered in the library, so I tried hard not to stare. As she found a good position, I thought of things she might say.

"Hi Gabrielle," I said, looking into those eyes, trying to act natural.

"Hi Cliff, how are you?" she said with an expression that she cared and wanted to know, which really threw me for a loop, and I paused.

"Oh, okay. I just helped a friend move, so I'm tired," I said, looking past her, to people going in and out Walgreens across the busy street, on their errands with bags in their hands.

"Stay, later, remind me, I've got a secret to tell you," she said softly. About then, the group wandered by, and she ran to join them with her friend laughing together, as if they had a private joke going on.

While I waited, time stood still in my mind as I wondered what she wanted to tell me. I had no clue. As the orange Frisbee orbited, and the dogs sniffed contents of the garbage cans for a hint of a meal, I sat there alone. I thought about David and how he was probably not worrying about what his mother might think of him now and how a little lie can grow and become bigger than the simple truth.

It was the start of a beautiful day with the sky-blue cerulean color that wove with the pure white cumulus clouds. I waited as the group went through their dynamics where one by one, each went a separate way to where it was down to Gabrielle who sat on a bench throwing peanuts to the pigeons.

My heart was pounding so that everyone should've heard it, and I got up, as natural as I could do under the circumstances. She had thrown a peanut to a lone pigeon and was stretching under her serape. I saw her young woman's figure there, and I almost took off with those voices in my head saying, *who am I trying to kid?* No, I thought interrupting them, she's got something that's important to tell me, and I'm going to hear it, so I walked to her bench, sat down.

"What a day," I said, begging the question on my mind.

"Ah," I started, trying to fill the silence, but she interrupted, putting her finger to her lips saying, "Ah," then she hesitated and the started, "about two weeks ago, I was driving in the snow by Alameda and I just happened to see you, walking with your head down, kicking through the snow. I saw you for that amount of time."

I thought back when everything had been going badly, surely, not one of my finest moments, by any stretch.

"And, as I saw you driving by, something happened," her voice trailed into an emotional tone. Suddenly she took my hand in hers, closed her eyes, and pressed it to her lips. "And it won't go away," And then she kissed me with her eyes closed, her lips soft against my hand.

My mind went blank, not ever thinking this would happen. I felt the velvet of her lips.She glanced at me to see my reaction and then got all embarrassed saying, "Well, Cliff, I gotta go now."

And then just like that, she was gone, as one her friends had waved to her whereupon she ran over to their ride, and she waved as they left. I waved back, still in shock over what had just transpired. I was left alone again, but my day had gone to crystal. The breeze ruffled the wafting leaves dappling the light. My day was now upside down, and I didn't know what to do,

A simple plan came to me. The next day was Sunday so I waited until church was over, and the clear ringing of the bells signaled mass was ending before I started my walk—the trip I'd made a thousand times, only now it was for real, as I headed west along San Francisco Street. The dappled shadows of the trees lent a slow-motion feel to my nervous steps, as the butterflies had begun fluttering. Her oval eyes, that kiss, found their way easily into my mind just enough so, that I knew she knew, that I was on my way.

Snatches of the stockade filled in my doubts but I walked on, trying to keep concentrating on the destination in my head. Before, I'd only gone to the part where Raul had stopped me with his stark warning. Only this time, I saw no other way, come what may on this day. Her features wove with the trees, sidewalks, and narrow alleys

"Next time, there will be blood," came to my mind but I had to ignore it.

I felt my stomach tighten, as here, I would retreat in my dreams, but not today, as I took a deep breath knowing I'd crossed it. The guards, that scene, her face kept going around in my head. Maybe, he's at church, only to have it dashed down.

Across the street that voice came, "I thought I had made it clear," Raul spoke with certainty, "that there was going to be blood." I got up and began walking across the quiet street. "*Ese*, I'm going to teach you a good lesson today," he head in my direction.

Just then, a car pulled into a drive across from where we were. A man got out and spoke in a voice I recollected vaguely. "Raul," he

250

interrupted, "what are you doing? This is the guy I told you about. You know, the one that helped Andrea when she got hurt on Juan's flatbed. He's the one."

Raul's countenance changed as he looked at Andrea's father, and took in what he was saying. "Are you sure?"

"Sure, how could I forget that?" he said, smiling.

"*Bueno*," Raul said, stopping in his tracks, taking a breath and looking at me. "This is your lucky day, gringo. I just happen to be Andrea's godfather. That changes things. You come by to see Andrea; Gabrielle too?" he beckoned me over. Raul had his hands on his hips, smiling. "Okay," he said, "it's cool." He walked back to his porch and sat down.

Andrea was happy to see me and showed me her scar, telling me her limp was getting better and how she could even run now. When she was done, I asked her, "Is Gabrielle home right now?"

She smiled and said, "Yes, we went to Mass a while ago.'

"Thank you, I'll be seeing you later," I said ,giving her a hug,

By the almost showdown I was spent, and then seeing Andrea, and I was worried that my energy wasn't right to make my visit. But I couldn't leave without seeing Gabrielle after going all this way. I took that big breath and approached the adobe house, feeling like I was made of jelly. I forced myself up that drive, over the sidewalk, and up to the wooden door and knocked.

It felt like eternity and nothing happened, until the door opened and a lady looked out saying, "*Que está, Señor?*"

In a shaky voice I said, "I'd like to see Gabrielle," seeing past her to Gabrielle, and in that slight tremble, I noticed as she reached for her purse, ready for a walk together. I knew, I knew, and then I looked into those eyes and nodded smiling.

EPILOGUE

And yet it was you too, Santa Fe my friend, day in and day out, walking your ancient sidewalks, searching your true beauty of sudden gentleness, weaving words in my notebook to describe you, discovering from what was always there inside that wouldn't let me down in spite of myself. Through the pen's magical key in the inevitables that rhymed with my thirst, held to this need that the words were in my blood ,for my call out as far as just being able to make it back, never once questioning all the if's and maybes that burned in the days under the azure blue. Unforsaken in the meanings, so the fire burned—that it wasn't so much to the truth to it all or the flung out openness edged in desperation that paced up and down in the middle of the night, straining for the images to get that right one that would open the next phrase clean with insight.

And yet, Santa Fe, you were as much a part of it all with your freedom midst the clashing culture's truce, where artists forged respect for the individual, to walk crazy as the contradictions that drove me til weary insight, with the last straw realized around simple people who saw through the veneer to what was inside of me was more than I thought. Like the times I slept in front of Norm's heater after reading poetry late into the syllabled night, only to wake up to a certain shade of morning grey that told me I had just enough time to make it to the Pantry Restaurant to get the dishes done, never thinking as I sorted the forks and spoons that all of this might be a grand illusion connected to you in sound that claimed its right.

Santa Fe raw as the wind-souled mirror myself, mixed with the features that I loved to walked within, as the converging worked in this turmoiled me, for that brief time never again to be the same. A style emerged independent of myself where images out of the ordinary spoke for themselves, motioned thus impressioned in this conscious ply in their own ways, falling to the page to do battle. Walking those streets with my Rainbow Bread bag tucked under my belt. The notebook and Bic pen never far from me of those days that spun alive, when all I had was what words held of this life and the sounding vision that ran their edges deep. Not always coming at once, some never quite right, yet same as this now through this ballpoint to you. What it was about you and your streets and that time, mystery of it all, in your whispers that sifted my talent that I heard in the moments ,coming ahead of me just out of reach. So in me that season worked, and revolves in this now to its freedomed place, where revealing in the process claimed its prize in the firsts that cut the sound with beauty, pure in which now sets me free in this telling joy.

www.ingramcontent.com/pod-product-compliance
Lightning Source LLC
Chambersburg PA
CBHW051510120626
46551CB00012B/858